STRUGGLE TO BE THE SUN AGAIN

Introducing Asian Women's Theology

Chung Hyun Kyung

ORBIS BOOKS

Maryknoll, New York 10545

STRUGGLE TO BE THE SUN AGAIN

Seventh Printing, February 1997

The Catholic Foreign Mission Society of America (Maryknoll) recruits and trains people for overseas missionary service. Through Orbis Books, Maryknoll aims to foster the international dialogue that is essential to mission. The books published, however, reflect the opinions of their authors and are not meant to represent the official position of the society.

Library of Congress Cataloging-in-Publication Data

Chung Hyun Kyung.
    Struggle to be the sun again: introducing Asian women's theology
Chung Hyun Kyung.
        p.   cm.
    Includes bibliographical references and index.
    ISBN 0-88344-684-7
    1. Feminist theology.   2. Theology, Doctrinal — Asia.
3. Liberation theology.   I. Title.
BT83.C485   1990
230'.082 — dc20
                                                        90-42683
                                                           CIP

About the title:

The title of this book "Struggle To Be the Sun Again" comes from the poem, "The Hidden Sun," which is written by a Japanese woman, Hiratsuka Raicho. In her poem, she claims that "originally, woman was the sun. She was an authentic person. But now woman is the moon." That means once Asian women were self-defining women but now they have become dependent women defined by men in their lives. Therefore she perceives Asian women's struggle for liberation as "Struggle To Be the Sun Again." I think her poetic expression aptly shows Asian women's yearning for wholeness.

About the artwork:

The cover painting is done by Korean feminist theological artist, Kim Yong Lim.

To My Three Mothers

Oh Yang Kwang (1915-   )
  Mother who gave me birth

Kang Du Ran (1908-1982)
  Mother who gave me milk

Chang Won (1915-   )
  Mother who gave me honey

CONTENTS

PREFACE

Writing this book was like a long journey home. On the road I met many suffering Asian women whose pain made me see my own wounds, and their struggle for liberation empowered me to actively seek my own and my Asian sisters' healing. I also met many strong, wise Asian women whose power and wisdom inspired me to believe in my own and other Asian sisters' power and wisdom. It was a journey full of agony and beauty. I agonized because my own self-hate and self-doubt had blinded me so I did not see the birth of my own and my Asian sisters' emerging new theologies. I also celebrated my own and my sisters' beauty when my self-hate was transformed into self-love through the discovery of life-giving truths among Asian women. Finally, I feel I have come home because I am at home with myself and have found a home in Asian women's struggle for full "womanity."

This book is about emerging Asian women's liberation theology. I intend to present the context and specific contributions of emerging Asian women's theology out of their struggle for survival and liberation. I approach Asian women's storytellings, poems, and theological writings like a painter who is witnessing the eruption of a volcano and wants to let other people know that the volcano is exploding. Because of the urgency of the eruption, constantly moving and changing, I have drawn a rough sketch of the volcano with large, fast strokes; I have not always been able to convey the subtle differences in shape, color, and texture of this historical eruption among long-silenced Asian women. Often I think the erupting volcano in my drawing looks oversimplified and generalized. Yet I believe it catches the momentum of the eruption with accuracy in its broad picture.

With shyness and trembling I share my rough sketch of the unfinished eruption with my Asian sisters and those others who can make connections between their own and Asian women's struggle in this world. I hope my drawing will generate some stirring of the heart, sharing, discussion, fighting, laughter, and celebration among people who are traveling on their own journeys home.

Many people touched me in my long journey. They listened to my sometimes incoherent talk, fed me with the food of friendship, and embraced me when I needed Mommy so that this lonely and difficult journey was bearable to me.

First of all, I would like to express my sincere appreciation to four members of my Ph.D. dissertation committee at Union Theological Seminary in New York City. They nurtured my intellectual growth and their support enabled me to transform my dissertation into this book. James Cone, my major advisor, encouraged me to write my dissertation about "something which hurts you the most." He also criticized me, saying, "Get out of your 'sin of profoundity.' Trust Asian women's theological wisdom and describe it simply and plainly. But if you really want to voice the struggle of the poor, never present it poorly." I thank Dr. Cone for his guidance, understanding, and love of my people. Beverly Harrison and her work, especially her article "The Power of Anger for the Work of Love," brought me to Union Theological Seminary. Her presence in my Union days always reminded me I had to take my anger seriously and channel it not at myself, but use it to enhance my "passion for justice." Kosuke Koyama motivated me, especially through his spirited disagreement with many points in my dissertation, to clarify my Asian identity in its ever-increasing complexity. His challenge led me to rethink the meaning of Christianity in the Asian context. Letty Russell from Yale Divinity School supported me through her ongoing personal connections with many Asian women and her diligent reading on Asian women's emerging theologies. Her sisterhood and solidarity with Asian women, especially her loyal support to the Asian Women Theologians group in North America, empowered my journey.

Provocative discussions with many Asian and other Third World people in theology, who gave me their precious time for interviews, stimulated my theological growth. I thank many Asian sisters: Lee Oo Chung, Cho Wha Soon, Lee Sun Ai, Chung Sook Ja, Kang Myung Soon, and Sohn Eun Ha from Korea; Aruna Gnanadason from India; Marlene Perera and Bernadeen Silva from Sri Lanka; Elizabeth Tapia, Lorretto Mapa and Virginia Fabella from the Philippines; Kwok Pui-lan from Hong Kong; and Nantawan Boonprasat Lewis from Thailand.

I also thank Asian male theologians and other Third World theologians who gave their insight through interviews: Hyun Young Hak, Ahn Byung Mu, Suh Kwang Sun, Kim Yong Bok, and Park Sang Jung from Korea; Tissa Balasuriya, Aloysius Pieris, and Preman Niles from Sri Lanka; M. M. Thomas, Samuel Rayan, and K. C. Abraham from India; Yeow Choo Lak from Singapore; and Mercy Amba Oduyoye from Ghana.

I am very grateful for the support of my teachers and colleagues at Ewha Women's University in Seoul, Korea, especially my former advisor Park Soon Kyung. I am deeply thankful to my colleagues at the Women's Theological Center: Donna Bivens, Nancy Richardson, Francine Cardman, and the 1988-89 study/action participants.

Precious friends kept me sane. In Boston, Angelica and Richard Harter gave me a sanctuary to live and write while I was finishing up my dissertation. Patricia McCullum fed me with Asian food and her feminist spirituality. Kim Hae Sun reminded me that I was born to dance. Barbara Brockelman midwifed the birth of my Goddess. My editor, Thomas Holt, painstakingly and respectfully reconstructed my Korean-English into something communicable.

My friends from Union Theological Seminary, whom I left behind while I wrote my dissertation in Boston, dreamed about my defense and sent me their energies through the telephone and beautiful cards. They are Ada María Isasi-Díaz, Marilyn Legge, Pamela Brubaker, Elizabeth Bounds, Lois Kirkwood, Sallie McNickle, Dwight Hopkins, and Howard Wiley. I especially thank Korean students at Union for their support. My three Korean feminist friends in New York have been a continuous inspiration: Shin Hae Soo, Rew Sook Ryul, and Lee Sung Ok. I celebrate their commitment to Korean women's struggle, diligent study and work, and their raw, wild Korean women power.

Finally I would like to express my appreciation to my husband, Chun Sang Kyung, for his generosity and understanding. He was willing to support my eight-month "leave of absence" from being a wife.

Returning after eight years to my motherland, Korea, was a great joy to me. Now is the time to "de-educate" myself from the Western theological training and to be "re-educated" by the spiritual wisdom of my people, especially my foremothers. I envision myself as a young tree who has sunk her roots deeply into the rich soil of mother earth and who drinks water from the well of my people's history and culture. In my divided motherland who cries for unification, I celebrate the power of my strong mothers. Remembering them, I humbly dedicate this book to my three mothers: Oh Yang Kwang, who gave me birth; Kang Du Ran, who raised me; and Chang Won, retired from the faculty of Ewha Women's University, who guided me spiritually through my college years in Korea. Their blood and flesh, milk and honey, gave me the courage to dream, risk, and heal.

Chung Hyun Kyung
August 15, 1989
Ewha Women's University
Seoul, KOREA

INTRODUCTION

Doing theology is a personal and a political activity. As a Korean woman, I do theology in search of what it means to be fully human in my struggle for wholeness and in my people's concrete historical fight for freedom. By discerning the presence and the action of God in our midst, I want to empower my own liberation process as well as that of my community. Our personal stories of agony and joy, struggle and liberation are always connected with our socio-political and religio-cultural contexts. Theology, therefore, is a discourse both intimate and public.

My theological questioning neither falls from the sky nor is derived primarily from the academy. Rather, it comes from my anger and hope as a Third World woman who refuses to be victimized by any kind of colonialism. My theology is also inspired by my burning desire for self-determination, and it originates from a liberation-orientated, Third World interpretation of people's history.

The two most significant events which shaped my theological perspective were my exposure to the Korean student movement and my discovery of the surrogate mother who gave birth to me. The merging of these two events in my personal history empowered me to listen to the cries from my people and from my innermost self.

The Korean student movement opened my eyes to the reality of Third World-ness. For the first time in my life, through the movement, I felt proud of coming from an economically deprived family. Before I entered college and was introduced to the movement, I was always ashamed of the lack of money and resources in my family and the way I looked. I was a skinny, dark, very flat-nosed and round-faced girl. I felt I was not pretty by the way people looked at me.

From the age of ten, the year my father lost all his wealth through bankruptcy, all my daily efforts were geared toward getting out of the poor neighborhood where I lived. I missed my former affluent neighborhood where I once enjoyed the best of material comforts. In that neighborhood everything seemed clean. Flowers bloomed throughout the year. Children did not use vulgar words. The whole environment seemed beautiful and pleasant. To be removed and placed in a poor neighborhood was indeed "paradise lost" to me. Throughout my adolescence I was a strange little girl who did not want to identify with the poor people around me. I studied very hard in order to get out of the ghetto and return to the place of my birth and early childhood. With iron determination I succeeded in entering the most prestigious high school in Korea, a springboard to upward mobility in Korean society. Not surprisingly, the majority of students who entered the school came from privileged families. However, they did not look like people from "paradise" to me any more. I did not feel close to them. Their arrogance and apparent unawareness of their privilege created an unbridgeable gap between them and me. Even though we all wore uniforms, our class backgrounds were clearly visible by looking at the content of our lunches. I suffered every lunchtime. I could not understand why many of them ate American ham and cheese and other foreign foods every day. I could not understand the big economic gap between them and me. I thought they were lucky to have rich parents, and I was unfortunate because my parents became poor. I questioned the fairness of God. I could not understand why God allowed certain people so much wealth, but not my family and others like us.

Extreme competition in the school dehumanized all of the students. The major focus in the curriculum was learning mathematics, English and other foreign languages such as French and German. Good grades automatically led us to good colleges. We fanatically memorized the foreign vocabularies and mathematical formulas like robots so we could get good grades. It was a long and lonely adolescence.

With many unresolved questions and repressed, unnamed anger, I went to college and was exposed to the student movement. It was a salvation experience for me. In small study groups outside of the university I learned the nature of colonialism and neo-colonialism, which were the causes of the chronic suffering of our people. I began to realize that the poverty around me was not the result of bad luck or laziness but due to unequal power relationships among people, institutions, and nations.

I was happy that my country was not the cause of other people's suffering, like many of the North Atlantic countries that exploited the countries of the South. I was proud that I could be one of the voices from the Third World trying to expose and dismantle the evil of colonialism. Many of us who were influenced by the student movement wanted to uncover the lies created by foreign and domestic power elites. We realized that our own understanding of our people, our history, our culture, and even our beauty standards were distorted primarily by Japanese colonial power and neo-colonial manipulation of the United States.

We also questioned everything about the role of institutionalized education, mass media, government, military, laws, and the mode of production in our country. The more we studied and experienced the Third World reality of our country, the more we understood how much we were brainwashed by political and cultural imperialism from First World countries. We raised radical questions about the web of the power structure around us. We knew that "the master's tools will never dismantle the master's house."[1]

Many of us became experts in the "hermeneutics of suspicion."[2] We did not believe what ruling authorities said in various parts of the world. Rather, we investigated what they were doing in power relations in order to determine who benefited from what they said and did.

My Third World awareness led me to question the colonialism and neo-colonialism in theology. Throughout my formal theological education in Korea, I was taught all about the European theologies of Schleiermacher, Barth, Tillich, Bultmann, Moltmann, and Pannenberg, the so-called theological giants of the nineteenth and twentieth centuries. I was not taught anything about Korean people and their theological reflections on Korea's history and culture. My learning in the university, therefore, did not help me to discern the activity of God in my people's everyday struggle in Korea. Instead, it was the student movement that enabled me to see the false ideology embedded in my formal theological education. Deconstruction of every aspect of theological imperialism became a main focus in my theological work. I decided that I would not waste my life solving the theological puzzles of the people who were the cause of our suffering; I wanted to spend my energy debunking their theological imperialism and studying Asian people's history and culture as I listened to my people's inner voice in their struggle for survival and liberation.

However, when I look back on my theological search today, I must confess I have spent most of my theological education reacting against white European and North American theologies, trying to name the colonial and neo-colonial ramifications of their discourse. I have hardly found the time and energy to construct my own theology in white academic settings. I realized clearly that reacting against the oppressive system would not necessarily lead me to constructing a liberating reality. I learned the hard way that I had to get in touch with the power and the history of myself and my people in order to find and construct a new, liberating reality.

The watershed event that helped to shift my theological direction existentially from deconstruction to reconstruction was my discovery of the woman who gave birth to me. She was a Korean version of a surrogate mother. When I visited Korea during the summer of 1987 for my doctoral research, I discovered for the first time the existence of my biological mother. I had always thought the parents who raised me also gave birth to me. No one in my family had mentioned her existence to me. Since all the public documents about my birth were manipulated by my father, my birth mother became a "no-name" woman, totally erased from my family's private and public life. Even when my parents died, they did not mention her to me in their last words.

The person who resurrected my biological mother in my personal life was my cousin. She knew the well-kept secret of my birth. At the time of my birth she lived with my parents, helping with housework. In return she received shelter and food from my parents. Since her father was a poor fisherman in a small island in Chunla province in Korea, he sent his little daughter to his well-off brother in the city. During this period my father had some political and economic power in the city. He wanted to have his own child but his wife could not conceive. After twenty-five years of waiting, my father decided to find a woman who could conceive for him.

The woman who gave birth to me was a poor single mother who was living with her only son in my father's city of Kwang Ju. She lost her lover during the Japanese colonization of Korea. My birth was a great joy to her. It was, however, also a great sadness. She had to give me up to my father and the woman who became my new mother. They took me from my birth mother on my first birthday. My mother did not want to let me go. She knew, however, that she could not fight against my father and new mother. They were powerful people; she was powerless. My birth mother cried over my departure at the railroad station on a rainy spring day about thirty-two years ago. Soon after, she became mentally disordered due to her great sense of loss. Her only son, who was a teenager at that time, could not bear his mother's suffering and committed suicide.

In Korean society, which is strongly influenced by Confucian law, women who give birth out of wedlock are ostracized. No law, custom, or community structure protects them. They are treated as outcasts. The social message is that these women should feel ashamed of themselves. The social ostracism they go through does not stop in their generation. It passes on to their children. In the Yi dynasty, which lasted until the dawn of the twentieth century in Korea, children of a surrogate mother could not take exams to hold governmental offices.[3] This tradition still thrives in Korean society today, although in a subtle way. My birth mother wanted to protect me from social ostracism. She placed me in the category of a "normal, legitimate" child by erasing her very existence as a human being and pretending that I had not been born from her womb. I can see many nameless crucified people in my birth mother.

When I first went to meet my birth mother and listened to the stories of her hard life's journey, I felt that something in my deepest being was broken open. It was like the experience of baptism: something was washed away and I felt truly free. Through this ill, seventy-two-year-old woman, my mother, I felt that I was encountering the power of the despised in my people's history. "Hyun Kyung," I said to myself, "you have studied theology for more than eleven years. For whom have you done your theology? Why did you want to do theology? You always thought you studied theology in order to empower the oppressed people in your country. But face it! Have you really paid attention to the culture and history of the poor in the development of your theology? Have you been willing to learn from them? With whom have you spent most of the time in order to formulate your theology—the poor or the intellectuals in academia? You have tried so hard, consciously and unconsciously, to prove yourself, your intelligence, to the dominant theological groups using the language of those very groups."

I felt ashamed of myself, of my hidden desire to be better than the dominant theologians of Europe and North America. I felt an inner, powerful spirit turning me from my wish to do theology like Europeans and toward the open arms of my mother, where I could rest safely in her bosom. There was no turning back, and I felt a strong existential urge to cross and then destroy the bridge called theological higher education, which stood between "them" and "me." Then I looked at my mother. My sobbing mother looked like an icon of God through which I could clearly see what God was telling me about my mission.

To meet this woman, my birth mother, opened another dimension of my theological consciousness. Several theological questions I struggled with theoretically became existentially clear to me. Encountering my mother helped me to identify my theological concerns, especially as they relate to the norm and sources of Third World women's theology. As I listened to my mother's life story—her struggle for mere survival in this unfriendly world—I was angered by "the culture of silence" in which she lived.[4] People around her silenced her in every way. Without any system of support to be a productive and public person, the only way she could survive without being mutilated was by becoming totally invisible. However, "silence never protected her."[5] Her heart was broken; she was forced into poverty, and for a period of time became mentally disordered.

Throughout my eleven years of theological training, I have written countless term papers and theological essays for highly educated people who were my teachers. The style and content of my speaking and writing have been shaped in such a way that persons like my mothers could never understand what I was saying. The more I become a "good," "professional" theologian, as defined by European and American theological scholarship, the more I become alienated from my mothers and people like them. Now it has become clear to me that I no longer want to write so-called "comprehensive" theology seeking to answer questions of privileged Europeans. I want to do theology in solidarity with and in love for my mother so as to resurrect crucified persons—like her—by giving voice to their hurts and pains, especially those Asian women who are located on the "underside of the underside of history"[6] in a white, capitalist, male-dominated world.

To choose the despised women of Asia as the primary context for my theology means to do theology that is accountable to their experience. Theological languages, paradigms, and questions that come from the life experiences of Western male intellectuals, who are the brains of the cultural hegemony which reduced poor Asian women to the status of non-persons, cannot serve as a source of Asian women's theology. The resources for Asian women's liberation theology must come from the life experiences of Asian women themselves. Only when we Asian women start to consider our everyday concrete life experiences as the most important source for building the religious meaning structures for ourselves shall we be free from all imposed religious authority.

We Asian women must trust our own feelings and judgments and use them to challenge the established norms which designate what is right and wrong or what is good and bad. Our concrete, historical, everyday, lived experiences must serve as the final test of our theology. If a religious teaching or practice provides a life-giving power to Asian women so that we can sustain and liberate our lives, that teaching and practice becomes "good news"—gospel—for us. If it makes Asian women die both inside and outside, it becomes "bad news." Asian women's communities of resistance and struggle must define the meaning of our liberation and wholeness by ourselves.

This work is an interpretation of emerging Asian women's liberative consciousness. My purpose is to articulate the specific contribution of an emerging Asian women's liberation theology to the meaning of the gospel. What are the distinctive theological challenges of Asian women to theology and the church out of their struggle for survival and liberation? This is the question that I will seek to answer. I hope not only to identify the contributions of Asian women's theology but also to suggest the future directions it ought to take.

Since Asian women's theological writings with a feminist consciousness have only become visible in the 1980s, there have not been many research projects on Asian women's theology. Many individual essays on specific topics of Asian women's theology have appeared in various journals. However, detailed research is rare. There are two doctoral dissertations that are important. One is by Kwok Pui-lan of Hong Kong, and the other by Elizabeth Tapia of the Philippines.

Kwok Pui-lan, a lecturer of church and society at Chinese University in Hong Kong, completed her dissertation at Harvard Divinity School on the topic "Chinese Women and Christianity 1860-1929." Kwok's study focuses on emerging Asian women's feminist consciousness by looking at the impact of Christianity on Chinese women's lives. She also articulates the theological understanding of God, Christ, Mary, and other themes from Chinese women's perspective using many written materials from China and foreign mission boards. It is mainly a historical study which aims to reconstruct Chinese women's history during the dawn of the century. This study gives new insight on mission history in Asia.[7]

Elizabeth Tapia, a professor of social ethics at Harris Memorial College in Manila, completed her dissertation, "The Contribution of Philippine Christian Women to Asian Women's Theology," at Claremont Graduate School. In her research Tapia interviewed fifteen Filipino women from various social strata and theologically analyzed the meaning of full humanity for women and the significance of Filipino women's theology. She also analyzed the rise of many Asian women's theological organizations and their impact on the development of Asian women's theology.[8]

There are also some important books on Asian women's theology. Marianne Katoppo's *Compassionate and Free* is the first published book on Asian women's theology. Katoppo is an award-winning novelist and theologian from Indonesia. In her book she examines Asian women's situation through case studies and gives a theological reflection on Asian women's reality. She emphasizes Asian women's right to be "other" in relation to male domination and Western imperialism. She is searching for women-defined identity different from the ideal woman image of the dominant culture.[9]

Korean systematic theologian Park Soon Kyung, a former professor at Ewha Women's University, published two books on the relationship between Korean women's struggle and other Third World peoples' struggle. Standing firmly on neo-orthodox theological ground, she articulates the new meaning of Christ, Church, humanity, creation, and new theological methodology from Korean women's perspective. The titles of her two books are *Minjok Tongil Kwa Keedokyo* (*Unification of the Nation and Christianity*)[10] and *Hankook Minjok Kwa Yeosung Shinhak eu Kwajae* (*The Korean Nation and the Task of Women's Theology*).[11]

There are also important collections which have been published on Asian women's theology: *With Passion and Compassion*[12] from the Ecumenical Association of Third World Theologians; *Essays on Women*[13] and *Women and Religion*[14] from the Women's Studies Program of St. Scholastica's College in the Philippines; *A Hymn to Creation*[15] and *God, Women and the Bible*[16] from the Centre for Society and Religion in Sri Lanka; *Toward a Theology of Humanhood: Women's Perspective*[17] from All India Council of Christian Women; *The Context of Korean Women's Theology*[18] and *The Task of Korean Women's Theology*[19] from the Korean Association of Women Theologians; *Reading the Bible as Asian Women*[20] from the Women's Concerns Unit of the Christian Conference of Asia; and *We Dare To Dream: Doing Theology as Asian Women*, from Asian Women's Resource Centre.[21]

Important articles on Asian women's theology have been published by three major ecumenical magazines of Asia. *CTC Bulletin* of the Commission on Theological Concerns of CCA dedicated a whole issue on Asian women's theology.[22] *East Asia Journal of Theology* also had its special issue on Asian women's theology.[23] *In God's Image*, the only feminist theological magazine in Asia, has provided important essays on Asian women's theology.

Of the many articles by Asian women, Nantawan Boonprasat Lewis's article should be mentioned in relation to my research. Lewis is from Thailand and is now teaching at Metropolitan State University in St. Paul, Minnesota. In her article, "Asian Women's Theology: A Historical and Theological Analysis," she offers a valuable overview of Asian women's theology. She also clarifies the emphasis and methodology of emerging Asian women's theology.[24]

After an extensive survey of secular and theological literature on Asian women, I decided to focus primarily, though not exclusively, on the emergence of a feminist liberation-orientated theological consciousness among Asian women in three major settings: the Christian Conference of Asia (CCA), the Ecumenical Association of Third World Theologians

(EATWOT), and the Asian women's theological journal, *In God's Image* (*IGI*). I selected these three contexts because of their international focus, thereby encouraging the inter-connectedness and cross-fertilization in women's theological development. Each context has provided a place for women of many different Asian countries to dialogue and to support each other as they resisted a patriarchal theology, church, and society. In addition to the three main contexts, I will also use my own experience as a Korean woman and documents produced by the Korean Association of Women Theologians (KAWT). I will also draw on the wisdom of the theological writings created through All India Council of Christian Women in India and the Centre for Society and Religion in Sri Lanka.

The rise of a feminist liberation-orientated theological consciousness among Asian women is a recent development. In some Asian countries it began during the 1970s, and it occurred in the context of women's participation in political and theological liberation movements dominated by men. For example, the Korean Association of Women Theologians was initiated in 1980 by the Christian women who recognized sexism in the church and society through their experiences in the 1970s.

Although this book will use materials of women from national theological associations, its primary focus is international, that is, Asian women from different countries developing theology together with a feminist liberation orientation. The CCA, EATWOT and *IGI* are the best sources for an investigation of this nature. The primary materials for this work cover the period of the 1980s, the time when the theological consciousness of women in CCA, EATWOT, and *IGI* began to be expressed in published writings, conferences, and consultations.

My approach to the materials will be both historical and analytical. I will look at the historical development of Asian women's liberation theologies in relation to the development of the three organizations I mentioned and the Asian women's secular and religious liberation movement. I will also examine primary resources from Asian women's experiences with critical analysis. Since Asian women's liberation theologies are in the making, most of their materials are more descriptive or storytelling than analytical. I think it is necessary for Asian women's theology to go through analytical welding in order to discover the similarities and differences among them in the common work for liberation in solidarity. That will also help Asian women to move toward deeper self-understanding, stronger theological persuasion, and clearly directed praxis.

I will also use the oral histories of twelve Asian women, which I have collected through interviews. They are women who have played major roles in the development of Asian women's theology.[25] Also included are the interviews I conducted with fourteen Asian men and other Third World women and men in EATWOT, CCA, and related associations.[26]

This work is divided into seven chapters. Chapter 1 examines the historical origin of Asian women's theological consciousness in CCA,

EATWOT, and *IGI*. The primary concern is to show the contribution of these organizations to the development of Asian women's liberation theology.

Chapter 2 describes the social context of Asian women's theology, focusing primarily upon women's reaction to patriarchal values in the society, church, and family.

Four major theological themes have defined the development of Asian women's liberation theology. They are anthropology (Chapter 3), Christology (Chapter 4), Mariology (Chapter 5) and spirituality (Chapter 6).

In Chapter 7 I conclude by identifying the major contributions of Asian women's liberation theology and by suggesting the future directions it should take.

The significance of this work lies in its concern to give theoretical visibility to the struggles of Asian women. I will look at the emerging Asian women's theological voices from the "gender specificity" of their experience in order to pinpoint their distinctive struggle and the search for liberation in their Third World and Asian reality. Hopefully, my analysis may empower the liberation process of Asian women by naming the evil and envisioning the full humanity defined by Asian women themselves.

I hope that my book will also stimulate dialogue with other theologies from different contexts, particularly with Asian male liberation theologies and feminist theologies from the other parts of the world, by presenting the distinctive challenges from Asian women's liberation theologies. I hope the challenges will not stop at the level of dialogue but will move toward a liberation praxis in solidarity. Finally, my proposal for "survival-liberation-centered syncretism" as a new model for understanding Asian women's liberation theology may open the gate for the deeper understanding of God's activity in this pluralistic and divided world. I hope that my work will provide research that supports Asian women's struggle for self-determination, dignity, and wholeness.

1

THE HISTORICAL CONTEXT
OF ASIAN WOMEN'S THEOLOGY

Asian women's theology has been created out of the historical context of Asia's struggle for full humanity. The women of Asia awakened from their long silence and began to speak out in their own language about their experience of the divine.

Asian women's public visibility first occurred with the rise of the anti-colonial and nationalist movements in many Asian countries at the dawn of the twentieth century. Women fought alongside men to break the chain of imperialism and to recover the independence and self-determination of their countries. When women were politicized by their participation in the anti-colonial struggle, they also started to question feudalist, patriarchal customs and values in their respective countries. In many Asian countries the radical women's movement was suppressed after their independence until the 1970s. When many Asian societies had achieved relative peace due to independence, all other freedom struggles were subdued and women were encouraged to retreat into their homes. Recently, Asian women historians have uncovered these radical ideas on women's liberation, which originally developed during the period of decolonization.[1]

The present Asian women's movement, which is growing rapidly, in many cases has its origin in women's participation in the grassroots people's movement for "survival rights." National independence from the colonizers did not bestow a life of dignity to the majority of Asians. With the advance of neo-colonialism and dictatorships by a few local power elites, Asians suffered again under the turmoil of semi-feudalism, capitalism and militarism. But now the people have risen up again for self-determination and justice for all people. Women joined the movement for the survival of their community, and they discovered that fighting for male-defined justice would never provide a holistic liberation for women. Women began to organize their own groups in order to voice their concern for justice for themselves. This effort of women was encouraged by the United Nations' Declaration

11

of the Decade for Women (1975–1985) because the Declaration helped women's issues to gain greater public visibility.

The heightened consciousness on women's issues in secular society reached the church. Many theologically trained Asian women began to see that the church was the most anachronistic institution in their society. When the larger society started to change its overtly patriarchal practices due to pressure from the women's movement, the church tried to remain an "unchangeably divine" institution. Women as equal partners in Christ's mission were denied by the church in many ways, rationalized in the name of the revelatory truth of God in the Bible. Women were considered inferior to men; wives, therefore, were told to be submissive to their husbands at all costs. Women were regarded as unclean and lacking in will power — easy targets of temptation. Citing the Bible, many male clergy said that women should be quiet in the church; therefore women's ordination and public leadership were denied. If women wanted to be of any good, they should suffer as Christ suffered on the cross.[2]

Asian church women rejected this corrupted understanding of Christianity, as both unjust and unchristian. They began to reread the Bible from women's perspective and challenge the patriarchal biases of Christian theology and the church's practices.

Historically, Asian Christian women's theology arose with the help of three organizations which provide most of the material in this book: the Christian Conference of Asia (CCA), the Ecumenical Association of Third World Theologians (EATWOT) and the journal *In God's Image* (*IGI*).

The Women's Desk of the Christian Conference of Asia

After World War II many Asian countries were liberated from their colonizers. Political liberation brought two urgent tasks. One task, on a macro level, was the decolonization of the socio-political and religio-cultural institutions of the various Asian countries. The other task, on a micro level, was the reconstruction of the external and internal lives of individuals. The Christian communities of Asia, which were implanted from the West and dominated by Western missionaries, had to deal with the tasks their countries faced in order to be relevant to the people's struggle for full humanity. In this context the East Asia Christian Conference (EACC) was organized. (It was reconstructed with the name changed to Christian Conference of Asia [CCA] in 1973.) EACC had its first conference at Kuala Lumpur in 1959. Church leaders from many different Asian countries gathered together, clarified their Asian identity, and shared their struggles and hopes. EACC's main concern in this initial stage was nation building.

The most articulate voice at this historical stage was M. M. Thomas. According to Thomas, nationalism was "an essential preparation of Asia for the Gospel."[3] He made this point at the Inaugural Assembly of the EACC. Thomas claimed that the diverse religious and ideological groups of Asia could build a community together around the central concern of nation building. EACC responded positively to the rapidly growing nationalism in its member countries.

In the decade of the 1960s, EACC concentrated on the issue of indigenization. Many Asian theologians concluded that any meaningful theology in their setting had to be created out of their own cultural and religious heritages. In 1966 the EACC held its first conference for developing an indigenous theological dialogue.[4] The theological indigenization movement helped Asian theologians become sensitive to their own identity as Asians, in contrast to the identity given to them by Western missionaries. This was an affirmation of God's revelation through the indigenous religions and cultures of Asia. However, the limitation of their theological movement was soon detected. Theologians began to understand that their theological context was larger than the religio-cultural sphere. The theological context needed to include the totality of Asia's reality, especially the issues of human rights and justice within the secular, technological, ideological, and economic aspects of life for all Asian people. These efforts toward such a theological approach were called "contextualization." "Critical Asian Principles" became its theme.[5]

With the heightened theological sensitivity to contextualization and critical Asian principles, EACC/CCA's main theological concern was to articulate an Asian theology out of grassroots people's life experiences. Their theological efforts clarified the subject of theological contextualization. Asian theologians concluded that nation building and indigenization theology did not have clear class options. It was recognized that nation building in Asia did not benefit the masses but only a few power elites who had connections with the neo-colonial powers. It was also discovered that theological indigenization mainly dealt with the metaphysical so-called high religions of Asia from the texts and not with the living religions of the masses of the poor. Asian theologians realized that the subject of theology should be the majority of the people of Asia, who are poor. This new orientation was called the theology of the people.

All through these theological movements in CCA women's issues were never a central issue. In the late 1970s, however, many Asian Christian women began to see the need for a public channel in CCA through which women could speak out and be heard. Until then the CCA, which links seventeen Asian countries, had "programs on mission and evangelism, urban and rural mission, youth, development services and communications, but no programs on women."[6]

Under the pressure of women from many Asian countries, the Executive Committee of CCA hired Elizabeth Tapia of the Philippines in 1980-1981 to lay the groundwork for establishing a Women's Desk. Under Tapia's leadership two important meetings were organized: The Conference of Theologically Trained Women of Asia held in January 1981 at Subabumi, Indonesia, and The Asian Women's Forum held in May 1981 at Bangalore,

India.[7] These became the foundation for the Women's Desk in CCA.

Through the reports produced from these two important meetings Asian women made "their need of putting women's agenda in the structure and policies of the CCA [clear]."[8] When the Seventh General Assembly gathered in 1981 at Bangalore, women participants wrote and distributed leaflets on their concerns about justice for women, and the General Assembly of the CCA voted to establish the Women's Desk.

Mizuho Matsuda of Japan became the first executive secretary of the CCA's Women's Desk during 1982-86. In 1984 Matsuda organized a workshop on Asian women in the migrant situations under the theme "Asian Women's Reality, Poverty and Oppression." In this workshop Asian women encouraged one another to articulate women's situations in Asia from their Christian faith and to interpret the Bible with Asian women's specific life experiences. Out of this workshop the book *Reading the Bible as Asian Women* was produced.[9]

The CCA Women's Desk also published the consciousness-raising book *Women to Women; Asian Women in Solidarity: Mobilizing Women in Struggles for Food, Justice and Freedom.*[10] In the introduction of this book Matsuda eloquently expresses the goal of the CCA Women's Concerns Committee:

> We fight for women's positive participation in every aspect of life. We want women's perspectives to be considered in decision making. We support women doing things in their own unique way. However, women's struggles in Asia must not be seen in one dimension, as simply a struggle against men. It is vital to see the many aspects of the structural dimension (social, political, cultural and economic) which everywhere keep "the weakest" and "the least" in society—women as well as men—disadvantaged and deprived.
>
> Affirming the emphasis of the CCA Women's Concerns Committee for the next 5 years, women need to participate in the struggles for *Food, Justice and Freedom for ALL*. Struggle means awareness. Struggle means organization and unity. Struggle means courage, faith and hope. We must begin to build these up in our small circles and link up with one another. Nobody can help in this process more than women themselves. And, as Christian women, we must ask and find out what resources there are in our faith for this struggle.[11]

Offering the central place where Asian Christian women make connections among themselves for mutual support, the CCA Women's Desk made a crucial contribution to the development of Asian women's theology.

The Women's Commission of the Ecumenical Association of Third World Theologians

The Ecumenical Association of Third World Theologians (EATWOT) was established mainly by theologians from Asia, Africa, and Latin America to develop theologies "from the underside of history" that would critique and challenge the inadequacy of the dominant theologies from the First World and that would mutually support one another's efforts to do theology which would contribute to the liberation of the poor on their continents. The organizing Conference was held August 1976 in Dar es Salaam, Tanzania. Subsequent international conferences were held in Ghana in 1977, Sri Lanka in 1979, Brazil in 1980, India in 1981, Geneva in 1983 and Mexico in 1986.[12]

The organizing conference of EATWOT in Tanzania focused on the issue of the division among the rich and the poor and its implication for Third World theologians. What does it mean to do theology from the underside of history? How can Third World theologians develop the unity necessary to challenge First World theology? These were some of the central questions. It is noteworthy not only that women's issues did not become the subject of discussion, but also that only one woman was invited to this conference. Although Virginia Fabella of the Philippines did most of the preparatory work for the conference, she was not invited to the meeting because one of the male organizers thought she was not theologically equipped.[13]

The second EATWOT international conference was held in Accra, Ghana. It was a pan-African meeting focusing on the development of an African theology. Unlike the first EATWOT conference, more women were present. They introduced the contradiction of men talking about liberation in general but having great difficulty in addressing women's liberation in particular. For example, Mercy Oduyoye of Ghana pointed out African men's "irrational fear of blood (menstruation)," which made African women excluded from religious practice. Two other African women, Rose Zoe-Obinga of Cameroon and Constance Baratang Thetele of South Africa, also shared their experience as women. The presence of these three strong African women at the conference raised some women's issues. The final statement from the conference stated:

> We recognize that African women have taken an active role in the Church and in shaping our history. They have shown themselves to be an integral part of the liberation struggle. But we cannot ignore their exclusion from our past theological endeavors. The future of African theology must take seriously the role of women in the doing of theology.[14]

The third international conference of EATWOT was held at Wennappuwa, Sri Lanka in 1979. It focused on the development of an Asian theology.[15] The percentage of women participants was larger than at Accra; however, out of many public presentations, women took part in only one. The most significant progress on women's theology at this EATWOT international conference was an essay written from a specifically feminist perspective by Marianne Katoppo of Indonesia. Her paper, "Asian Theology: An Asian Women's Perspective,"[16] started with her personal experience as an Asian woman and ended with her claim to Asian women's right to be free from both Western and men's control.

In the final statement of the Asian conference the participants recognized the oppression of Asian women who endured the multifaceted oppression of Asian cultures and religions, lower wages, and prostitution accelerated by sex tourism. They perceived male domination in many aspects of women's lives. But Rose Zoe-Obinga, who participated in both the African and Asian continental meetings, remarked negatively on the conferences due to their gender exclusiveness. She pointed to the gap between the recognition of women's being oppressed and the praxis for real change in both Africa and Asia. She emphasized the need for more decision-making power for women. She said, "Liberation requires that the oppressed find their own words to name their own world."[17]

At EATWOT's fourth meeting at São Paulo, Brazil, the concerns of women's particular oppression seemed to take a step backward. Some women participants felt that the marginalization of their issues was due to the influence of male-interpreted Marxist ideology upon Latin American liberation theology. For example, Cora Ferro, a woman theologian from Costa Rica, criticized the oppression of women by the macho bourgeois ideologies of Latin American males and the lack of awareness of sexism in leftist ideologies.[18] From this perspective sexuality was tacitly considered a woman's private affair, not to be discussed openly (but still in reality to be exploited). Latin American women participants also criticized male liberation theologians: "In the area of theology the participation of women as active subjects of systemic work has been denied. By male standards the worth of a person is judged in terms of what that person knows in male terms."[19] Latin American women are present in the church *en masse*, but they are absent in the orientation and management of the church. Latin American women urged Latin men to see the interconnections of the oppressions of classism, racism, and sexism.

The Third World women's critique of Third World theology reached its peak at the fifth EATWOT international conference in New Delhi, India, in 1981. In "Reflections from a Third World Woman's Perspective: Women's Experience and Liberation Theologies," Mercy Amba Oduyoye named women's struggle for liberation as "the irruption within the irruption" of the poor in the Third World. She said that many male liberation theologians still thought inclusive language was a "big joke" and women's issues were peripheral to their work as liberation theologians.

It was such language [sexist] that sparked off the feminism discussion at Delhi. Yet more glaring perhaps was the fact that none of the formal papers was assigned to a woman. Presumably we were dealing with more "central issues," which, until Delhi, did not specifically include sexism and therefore no "competent" women could be discovered.[20]

According to Oduyoye EATWOT was a virtually male enterprise until Virginia Fabella undertook the assignment of program coordinator. At the Delhi meeting Oduyoye pointed out the oppression of women by male liberation theologians:

> There have been several international meetings at which Third World representatives have said that antisexism is not their priority. At times they have even said it is not an issue in their world, where men and women *know their place and play their role* ungrudgingly and no one feels suffocated by society's definition of femininity and masculinity. Issues of sexism are supposed to belong to a minority of disgruntled, leisure-saturated, middle-class women of the capitalist West. The few Third World women who speak that language are just allowing themselves to be co-opted. The fact is that sexism is part of the intricate web of oppression in which most of us live, and that having attuned ourselves to it does not make it any less a fact of oppression.[21]

After women's severe criticism of sexism in EATWOT, the organization acknowledged the fact that "the common human *experience of women* in their liberation struggle constitutes a true *source* of theology."[22]

The sixth EATWOT conference at Geneva, Switzerland, in 1983, a conference between First World and Third World theologians, was a step forward in the effort to overcome sexism in the organization. First and Third World women theologians found they had much to share concerning women's experience of sexism in their own contexts. Yet it was difficult, owing to their different socio-historical backgrounds, for women at the conference to set "the common agenda behind which they could unite to challenge the men's interpretation of theology."[23] It seemed necessary to have more meetings and dialogue before a provisional agreement between First and Third World women could be reached. When it came to defining their agenda, women from the Third World did not want to be controlled by First World women or Third World men. The final statement of the meeting illustrates this point:

> The oppression of women is a stark reality in the Third World where many cultures are strongly patriarchal. But to what extent this is an issue for Third World women is to be determined by the Third World women themselves. Neither Third World men nor First World women can determine the Third World women's agenda. Third World women maintain that sexism must not be addressed in isolation, but within the context of the total struggle for liberation in their countries.[24]

Third World women wanted to develop their theologies independently of Western theology, male liberation theology, and white feminist theology. They searched for organic methodologies and categories from their life experiences. During the sixth EATWOT meeting Third World women theologians decided to claim a space of their own where they could theologize authentically. A concrete plan was then established to support women's struggle for equality by the establishment of:

1. A working commission and coordinators on the continental level;

2. International Dialogues with special groups;

3. An intercontinental conference and assembly at the end of the next five-year period.[25]

EATWOT's executive committee approved the project of establishing a women's commission within the organization. The main purpose of the commission was to carve out a liberation theology from Third World women's perspectives.

During 1984-85 Third World women theologians held *women-only* national meetings in each member country, and then during 1985-86 held continental meetings in Asia, Africa, and Latin America. An intercontinental gathering was held in Mexico in 1986.[26] A consultation with minority women from the United States was held in May 1989 and a consultation with white women from the First World is scheduled in the near future.

EATWOT's women's commission has given Asian women a space to share their theological struggles and hopes. Many Asian women's theological writings have been stimulated and supported by EATWOT women's conferences. Three women have been crucial for promoting women's theology in Asia. Mary John Mananzan, dean of St. Scholastica's College in the Philippines, served as program coordinator for EATWOT. Lee Sun Ai of Korea, editor of *In God's Image*, acted as coordinator of the Women's Commission for the Asian continent. Virginia Fabella, former executive secretary of EATWOT, served as liaison between the Women's Commission and the EATWOT executive committee.

The Women's Commission also suggested topics for reflection:

1. Various oppressions of women and women's response
   a) in society
   b) in the church
2. Social analysis of their respective countries
   a) economic structure
   b) political situation
   c) socio-cultural and religious situations
3. Theological reflections
   a) Hermeneutical analysis of the Bible and other sources such as myths, folklore, legends, and indigenous religions
   b) God-talk and women
      Christology and women
      Mariology and women

Pneumatology and women
Emerging forms of spirituality[27]

Christian women in six Asian countries carried out their national consultations on feminist theology during 1983-85. They made much effort to include and to dialogue with grassroots women in their countries. They were challenged by the power and the depth of spirituality of these women, which enabled them to survive and to resist oppression. During November 21-30, 1985, Asian women gathered in Manila for their first continental meeting. The twenty-seven church women from seven Asian countries (Hong Kong, Japan, Korea, Malaysia, Philippines, India, and Sri Lanka) shared social and theological reflections from their respective countries and were empowered by one another.[28]

The majority of the women present were Protestant. The theme of the consultation was "Total Liberation from the Perspective of Asian Women." Women at the Asian consultation reflected on the following topics: women's oppression — a sinful situation; God-talk and women; women and the Christ event; women and the faith community; women and Mary; and women and the Holy Spirit.

The methodology proposed by the consultation was contextual, inductive, and collective. Participants visited urban and rural areas of the Philippines and listened to women's stories of struggle. The participants then did social analysis together on Asian women's oppression. Out of a deeper understanding of the reality which places Asian women in bondage, the participants reflected on various theological topics. There were no individual presentations or speeches. All final reflections on the topics came from group discussion and were expressed in the conclusions participants wrote together.[29]

This consultation stimulated Asian women's theological imaginations and strengthened the bonds among women from different Asian countries. Through this consultation the EATWOT Women's Commission contributed to our theological growth. Third World-ness and women-ness together became the center of Asian women's theologizing without undermining each other. The consultation expanded Asian women's understanding of liberation theology through their collective theologizing as Third World women.

In God's Image: A Feminist Theological Journal in Asia

In God's Image is the only feminist theological journal in Asia that publishes women's essays without national or denominational restrictions. It produced its first issue in December 1982 and has become the vital center for Asian women's theological exchanges. The IGI started as an occasional journal, but now produces four regular issues a year. IGI was started by a "theologically trained housewife who refused to be wasted."[30] Lee Sun Ai — a poet, minister and theologian from Korea — became the founder and editor of *IGI* which she started in her living room in Singapore, both out of her anger toward the injustice experienced by Asian woman and her vision of an empowered Asian women's theology. Due to her status as a foreigner and international worker's wife (her husband had begun to work for the CCA, which was then in Singapore), she was denied permission to work in Singapore even though she was an ordained minister. Determined not to accept this situation, Lee initiated an independent study of feminist theology and visited many Asian countries. After a period of learning and traveling, she concluded that Asian Christian women needed a public channel through which they could connect with one another and share the struggle and wisdom of their movement. Lee first thought of an Asian women's occasional newsletter with some theological expression. This idea eventually led, with the support of a group of women in Singapore, to the more ambitious idea of a journal devoted to the development of Asian women's theology.

Since formal theological education has been virtually denied to Asian women, the establishment of a feminist theological journal in the early 1980s was indeed an act of faith; theology in Asia had always been created by elite, Western-educated males. Asian women generally have not had the equivalent education of their male counterparts; therefore the theological reflections of Asian women have often been trivialized by male theologians. Many Asian male theologians have been saying that they wanted to include women theologians in their theological projects but could not find anyone who was theologically "equipped." It has been difficult for women to be regarded as serious, competent theologians. Marianne Katoppo described the sexist attitudes of Asian male theologians in her writing:

A woman theologian is still regarded as either Heretical or Hysterical! If the first, she is figuratively burnt at the stake. If the second, people hasten to find her a husband![31]

IGI became a theological sanctuary where women who were theologically orientated could share their reflections on the spiritual dimensions of life without male censorship. The ad hoc editorial committee of *IGI*[32] described the purpose of the journal as follows:

We know that in other parts of Asia women are doing theology and we believe it is important that this thinking should be shared. This is the purpose of *In God's Image*—we would like it to be a forum through which Asian women can share their theological thinking. We introduce it to you as a first step in what we hope will be a growing medium of communication between theologically orientated women in Asia.

We are taking this step because we believe that women have been given the gift of sharing their dreams and visions, their thoughts and theories, their hopes and fears, their frustrations and joys, and by so doing supporting each other. This magazine can be the vehicle for all the forms through which Asian women are shaping their theology— articles and lectures, Bible study, programs, poems, pictures, prayers, songs, service. We hope that *In God's Image* will be a means through which the contribution of women to theological thought in Asia can be heard.[33]

The committee members did not want to create another conventional academic journal. Rather, they encouraged other Asian women to share "their reflection on what it means to respond to the gospel as Asian women."[34] The committee suggested concrete ways in which Asian women could participate in the development of the journal:

— introduce yourself and others you share with in your context
— tell us what you are doing and thinking, planning and hoping for
— send us any expression of your thought, individual or collective, which can be reproduced in *In God's Image*
— tell us of others to whom we can send *In God's Image*.[35]

From this humble beginning *In God's Image* has grown in depth and breadth. In May 1987 it had its first advisory meeting and developed clearer editorial plans for the future.[36] The advisory committee suggested that the journal have a more thematic approach; future issues would deal with the issues of prostitution, militarism, women and politics, women and development, and other issues. In the winter of 1987 Sun Ai and her husband, Park Sang Jung, the general secretary of CCA, had to leave Singapore and become reestablished in Hong Kong because the Singapore government accused CCA, *In God's Image*'s umbrella organization, of subversion. The advisory committee members expressed their sisterhood and solidarity by editing and publishing *IGI*. The September 1988 issue was prepared by Indian women with the leadership of Jessie Tellis-Nayak. The March 1989 issue was put together by Filipino women with the leadership of Virginia Fabella. Lee Sun Ai now works for the establishment of an Asian women's resource center where Asian women's writings on their lives can be honored and preserved for present and future generations of Asian women. In this way she envisions enhancing the richness of *IGI*.[37]

2

THE SOCIAL CONTEXT
OF ASIAN WOMEN'S THEOLOGY

Asian women's theology was born out of Asian women's tears and sighs and from their burning desire for liberation and wholeness. It is neither the logical consequence of academic debate of the university nor the pastoral conclusion of the institutional church. Asian women's theology has emerged from Asian women's cries and screams, from the extreme suffering in their everyday lives. They have shouted from pain when their own and their children's bodies collapsed from starvation, rape, and battering. Theological reflection has emerged as a response to women's suffering.

Throughout the long history of colonization, Asian women have cried out both openly and secretly as they confronted the injustices in their lives. Most of the time no one heard their cries. Seldom did Asian women hear words or experience deeds of comfort from male-dominated religions. Asian women's tears and sighs had been accumulated in their collective unconscious for thousands of years without many public channels for expression. As a consequence, today the pent-up anger is finally beginning to explode like a volcano with much fire and flame. They are challenging God, who Christians say loves everyone, about "his" silence. Asian women are asking, "*Where* were you when we were hungry? *Where* were you when we called your name as our bodies were raped, mutilated, and disfigured by our husbands, policemen and the soldiers of colonizing countries? Have you heard our cries? Have you seen our bodies dragged like dead dogs and abandoned in the trash dump?" Faith for Asian women has been difficult, because their lives have been filled with so much agony.

After many heartaches, Asian women are coming of age. They are becoming stronger and wiser. They no longer believe in an omnipotent, sovereign God who takes care of every agony in their lives, like a father or a big brother caring for a helpless little girl.[1] Like the God of their colonizers and the God of the dominant institutional church, "he" did not give them life-giving power. Instead, "he" accentuated their feelings of abandonment and helplessness like a judgmental father or brother who wanted to set an example for a bad girl: "See, as I told you, you should have been quiet, obedient, and dead! You should have heard what I said and done things the way I wanted them."

Asian women who have come of age refuse to be daddy's or brother's helpless little girl. They are determined to recover their full humanity and ripened "womanity."[2] They also are renaming their own God who gives birth to their dignity and nourishes and empowers them in their life struggle. They are searching for the God who is present among them and with whom they can share their tears and sighs. They want a "God who weeps with our pain."[3]

Asian women have begun to ask hard questions. They first ask *what* God is doing in their lives and *where* God is working. Their first question leads them to another question: *Who and what is God?* The question about God's action in their lives precedes the question about God's being or essence. Out of these hard questions, Asian women are trying to carve a theology that is "very Third World, very Asian and very women."[4]

Asian women's theology is "very Third World" because their reality is marked by poverty and oppression. Colonialism, neo-colonialism, militarism and dictatorship are everyday reality for most Asian women. When poverty strikes Third World people, the ones who suffer the most are women and children. They are also the majority of the population. When there are no material resources for survival, and many poor men have already lost their wills to continue their lives, most Third World women do not even have the luxury to give up their lives. They refuse to lose hope and die. They feel that they *have* to survive. They know their children will die from starvation if they give up life. They create food for life out of nothing. Their bodies take and carry all the burdens for survival. They choose life under the worst lifeless conditions in order to give life to their children. A Korean feminist sociologist, Sohn Duck Soo, describes this phenomenon movingly:

> The abyss between brutal social reality and motherhood creates frustration and "Han." "Han" is sadness and suffering. "Han" is, however, transformed to the power and hope for survival for the sake of the children who are the other self of mothers. . . . Mothers overcome pain and despair because of their love to children. Isn't the mother's love the power which endures all the oppression and poverty and enables whole humanity to survive?[5]

Third World women are the poor among the poor. They are, however, creators and sustainers of humanity, embracing all the miseries of Third World-ness in their bodies. Together with Asian male liberation theology, Asian women's theology is derived from this Third World reality of poverty and oppression.

Asian women's theology is also "very Asian." It embraces many different people and rich religious, cultural, and linguistic heritages. Asia encompasses 58 percent of the world's population and Asian women comprise one quarter of the world's people.[6] Asia is also the birthplace of all the great world religions. Christians in Asia are less than 3 percent of the population. The majority of Asians are Buddhists, Hindus, Muslims, Taoists, or Confucianists.[7] Asia, therefore, is a non-Christian continent.[8] Asian women's theology seeks to articulate the meaning of the Christian message "through the sources within its [Asia's] own millenia-old culture, and all the living faiths of its neighbours."[9]

Asian women's theology is also "very women." It is a theology articulated by women out of their specific experiences and questions. Asian women share all the blessings and the problems of being Asian and Third World people with Asian men. What distinguishes Asian women's struggle from the men of the continent is their women-ness. Asian women are oppressed economically, socially, politically, religiously, and culturally in specific ways just because they are women. They are naming this gender-specific oppression in order to liberate themselves from patriarchal bondages and achieve self-determination.

However, to construct theology according to Asian women's own terms is not an easy task. It is frequently criticized by Asian men, and even some Asian women approach it with ambivalence. Both reactions have something to do with negative attitudes toward the rise of feminism in North America and Europe. It has been said that the women's liberation movement and feminism in Asia are imported from white women's ideas in the capitalist West and have nothing to do with Asian women's reality. Any Asian woman, therefore, who raises her voice for the specific rights of women is open to the charge of being brainwashed by white feminists. The critics of the Asian women's liberation movement also label its advocates as family breakers and call them middle class, uninterested in the welfare of the poor masses of Asia.[10]

It is important to note that some Asian men are sympathetic to the Asian women's liberation movement. But even they often want to instruct Asian women by advising them to cherish an "Asian feminism" which is *not confrontational*. Other Asian men agree with Asian women's claims for women's rights. But they either give only lip service or ask Asian women to wait until men finish the nationalist revolution or class struggle.[11] These patriarchal ideologies, of course, make the advocates of Asian women's liberation angry and frustrated. Some groups of Asian women have responded to their critics in collective written reports. The following are examples of their responses.

Q. Isn't feminism a white women's notion from the capitalist West and therefore quite irrelevant to Asian women's reality?

A. This question has been raised often by men (and some women) in the society at large and in the church, which do not want to take the challenges from the women's liberation movement seriously. They undercut the legitimacy of women's claim for human rights in the name of nationalism, class struggle or whatever ideology will help them keep the patriarchal status quo. It is obvious that the term *feminism* originated from the capitalist West. But Asian women nonetheless rightly contend that the liberative core of feminism cannot be automatically despised merely because of its geographical origin. Asian antagonists should ask which kind of feminism they are talking about. The definition of feminism varies "because feminism is based on historically and culturally concrete realities and levels of consciousness, perceptions and actions."[12] At a recent Asian feminist workshop, women from Bangladesh, India, Nepal, Pakistan, and Sri Lanka defined feminism today as "an awareness of women's oppression and exploitation in society, at work, and within the family, and conscious action by women and men to change this situation."[13] Asian women define what feminism is for themselves and in their own concrete historical situation. If people can accept the fact that Christianity in Asia still has some liberative power in spite of its Western, missionary, and colonial background because Asian Christians rediscovered its liberative core, then they should be able to accept the liberative core of feminism rediscovered by Asian women. Some South Asian women have exposed the fallacy of those who reject feminism as Western but freely accept so many other Western products:

> These same people do not question the foreign origins of the parliamentary or presidential systems for instance; of the development of capitalism; of private ownership of land and absentee landlordism; or of the ideology of the Left. Granted that the term "feminism" was not born in South Asia; but then neither were the industrial revolution, Marxism, socialism, or for that matter, even some of our South Asian religions. Einstein was not born in Lahore, Marx in Calcutta or Lenin in Dhaka; yet their western origins have not made their ideas irrelevant for us. Nor should they be confined within national or geographic boundaries.[14]

Asian women are not mere imitators of white women from the West. They have minds of their own. Some Asian men who claim that Asian feminists are brainwashed by white women presuppose the intellectual inferiority of Asian women in relation to white women. This illustrates that those Asian men are the ones who have internalized Western colonialism, and not Asian women. Asian men learned how to despise their own people of color (especially women) by imitating the values of their white masters. If white women can think for themselves, why not Asian women? Asian women do not fight for their liberation as women because they have been brainwashed like childish little girls by white women. Asian women fight for their rights because they experience the evil of patriarchy in their own family, church, and community, and they are determined to destroy it.

Q. Is not the Asian women's liberation movement a middle-class women's movement that does not contribute to the poor women's struggle?

A. This question has been raised by Asian male theologians and other intellectuals who want to discard the women's liberation movement. It has also been raised by some leftist men and working-class women. Asian feminists do not deny that middle-class women are important participants in their movement. However, feminists reject the assumption that to be middle class automatically means to be an enemy of poor women. The problem is more complex. Asian feminists do not trust Asian men who seem to delight in rejecting feminists simply because of middle-class status. Asian male critics themselves are often middle-class and appear comfortable remaining that way. To these men Asian feminists respond by saying, "Only if you discard your political, social, and cultural ideas with your middle-class status, might we take your comments seriously."

In contrast to middle-class Asian men, the challenge of some leftist men and working-class women has some validity, even though they do not describe the full picture of the Asian women's movement. In many Asian countries the women's liberation movement seems like a middle-class movement. There are some valid reasons for this impression. First, most women who have access to the media and publications are middle-class women. They are educated at various higher educational institutions and have learned how to use the languages of the public world defined by male scholarship. These women have had a chance to learn to excel using the rules of male intellectual games. They have also learned the former colonizer's language, which has become an official language in many Asian countries. In most cases that language is English. Grassroots women know only native languages and do not have a higher education. Therefore, grassroots women's chances of attaining visibility in the public world are much less than middle-class women.

However, there are thousands of women's groups in the working class raising women's issues throughout Asia.[15] In Korea the mainstream of the women's movement is formulated by the women workers' movement. Many middle-class Korean women in the movement acknowledge that the Korean women's movement should focus on the survival rights of poor women and the unification of Korea. Feminism is a radical critique of all kinds of hierarchical relationships, of which the most fundamental is the relationship between the ruler and the ruled. It enables middle-class women to see their privilege over working-class women and, as a result, become self-critical of their middle-class social location.

Q. Do not feminists divide Asian communities, which must be united for our national liberation?

A. Asian feminists love their communities. Most of us are mothers, wives, sisters, and daughters in Asian communities. Therefore, when we are accused of being community breakers by Asian men due to our claim for our rights, we get frustrated by their lack of understanding. Most of the time the frustration is expressed in the form of a love-hate relationship. We Asian women love Asian men because they share our common destiny and struggle as Asians. Asian men are our comrades in our common struggle for liberation from colonialism and neo-colonialism, which exploit and dehumanize Asian people—women and men, young and old. We Asian men and women *together* are Third World people who have been victimized historically and have been made poor by the power elites from inside and outside Asia. When our men—fathers, brothers, lovers, and friends—are persecuted by the power elites, military dictators, and colonial and neo-colonial personnel, we feel angry and our hearts ache. Our men's well-being is intrinsically related to our well-being. They are members of our family. We Asian women often say that we do not want any feminist revolution which does not include our men and children. On many occasions in our history Asian women fought battles alongside Asian men in order to defend our dignity as a community. There are countless examples of Asian women's participation in the struggle for nationalism, democracy, and socialist revolution. Asian women have been imprisoned and tortured, have bled and been killed with Asian men in order to bring justice and wholeness in our society. Therefore we feel closer to Asian men more than any other members of the human community because of our shared experiences of pain and struggle. We care about their well-being, and we want them to flourish with all of God's given potential in them.

We do not like it, however, when Asian men act as if they have the right to define women's liberation according to their interests and convenience. We hurt most when we are betrayed by our comrades whom we trust. We are not hurt much when we are accused of being community breakers by those power elites who are the cause of injustice in our community because we expect them to libel us anyway. Asian men in the liberation movement who accuse Asian feminists of being community breakers should ask themselves whether they blame poor factory workers or landless farmers as community breakers when they fight against their oppressors. Asian feminists respond to those so-called progressive men with much suspicion regarding the integrity of their liberationist claims. For example, some South Asian feminists have asked:

> Isn't it incredible that progressive people become champions of tradition only when it comes to women? We do not blame peasants and workers when they try to change the system; yet women who refuse to be confined, dictated to, and misused are blamed for creating disharmony. Isn't it rather the patriarchal social system which crushes women and their personalities that is responsible for creating disharmony, for breaking up families? . . . Peace and harmony can no longer be maintained at the cost of women. We cannot talk of democracy outside the family and yet allow male dictatorship inside it.[16]

Asian liberationist men who say that they believe in the meaning of total liberation should be more self-critical. What happened in the history of the Korean workers' struggle in relation to sexism is enlightening.

The Korean women workers' struggle has been one of the most persistent powers of resistance among the Korean people's movement.[17] Women workers have refused to compromise their claims for justice due to threats and appeasement from the government and business owners. Women workers say the reason for their uncompromising stand comes from their lack of privileges. Since they have not had the experience of having privileges over other people, it is easy for them to resist temptation. These women workers have fought the battle for workers' rights with male workers. But women workers have had to confront their male comrades when male workers do not want to share decision-making power with women workers. What happened at the Dong-il Textile Company in Korea shows who the real community breakers in the people's movement are.

Dong-il Textile Company is an export-oriented company. As in many other textile factories, the majority of workers are women. Behind the rapidly increasing gross national product (GNP) of Korea in the 1970s were many women workers who worked under miserable conditions in the textile companies. These companies provided the main materials for Korean export. At Dong-il Textile Company about 80 percent of the workers were women. Male workers originally led the union. Women workers' consciousness was raised by their participation in the labor movement, and they finally elected a woman as their union leader.[18]

Some of the male workers who belonged to the union would not tolerate a woman as head of the union, so they accepted money from the company and tried to destroy the woman-led union with the help of the police. Women workers were disillusioned by this betrayal by their male comrades and resisted. Some of the male workers and policemen threw feces and urine at the women. Some women workers were force-fed on feces and had their breasts smeared with feces. This did not weaken their resistance; rather, it made the women-led union stronger. When police tried to arrest them by force, women workers took off their clothes and protested naked. This symbolic action made a qualitative leap in the Korean women workers' movement. Cho Wha Soon, who staunchly supported the women workers, confessed that this event raised her and other women's consciousness as women.[19]

Before this event women workers did not pay much attention to the women's movement because they considered it a middle-class movement. But after the betrayal by their male comrades, they began to realize their need for liberation from sexism.

When men perceive women's liberation as a community-breaking activity, they define the meaning of community according to their own self-interest without considering women's vision of community. Two poems from Korean male workers show us two radically different manifestations of male consciousness regarding women. One sees women's liberation as an *integral part* of the total liberation process. The other sees women as a *means* of male liberation. The first poem was written by Park No Hai and is entitled "Darning a Bed Sheet."

Darning a bed sheet
washing underwear
I beat my shameful breast
Together we came home from the factory
My wife stayed up past midnight
washing dishes, cleaning house
putting everything in order
even the covers of the chili sauce pot
I used to give orders to her
Bring me food
Bring me water
Give me my clothes

With my colleagues
since I joined the labor union
I could look at myself
indulged in being served
in the name of a husband
in the same manner
of the haughty managers tyranical
I've been taught by the world
that a man gives orders
and a woman obeys them
I was exploiting my wife
a little by little
and I was an honest model worker

Organizing a labor union
I became aware
their praises and prizes
for being a model worker
are only the bell
hung on the tail of a cat
their talks of protection
of workers as family
are only a nice-looking sugar floss

I too was becoming a dictator
in my home
like the merciless pursuers

of profit I hate
who are decked up with
convenient theories
absolute authority
and what's called common sense
Deeper I became involved
our struggle made me see
I was discharging their rest
in my own daily practice

As much as the workers are not
productive machines of profit
my wife is not my handmaid
Husband and wife are loving friends
of equal stand
whose relationship is founded
on trust, respect
and democratic sharing

Waiting for my wife's return
from her late work
I darn our bed sheet
A painful awareness
comes through
as the needle
goes through my thumb[20]

Worker Park No Hai began to realize his own oppression of his wife through his participation in the worker's movement. He discovered that he was a dictator in his home. He exploited his wife as he was exploited in the factory. Then he changed his lifestyle. He started to do so-called women's work. He now darns a bed sheet and washes underwear because he realizes that his wife is not his handmaid and liberation had to be experienced in their family, too. He gives up his male privilege in order to find "a new mode of life in which he frees himself of the sin of domination, thus setting his wife free from her cultural chain."[21] His self-criticism makes him see the web of oppression and a new vision of the community where men and women lived in "trust, respect and democratic sharing." No Asian woman wants to break this community.

Another poem by an anonymous male worker shows that male liberation consciousness for the just society does not necessarily include the liberation of women. It is entitled "Our Stories for Us."

Give birth, sisters,
ten, twenty babies until they grow up

becoming bodies against bodies
guns and swords against guns and swords,
becoming dragon fighters.

Don't care about
dog dream, dragon dream[22]
daughters and sons.
Give birth, sisters,
fifty, hundred babies,
children with strong fists
children with loud voices
until they together become fire and a battle cry

Don't care about
musty genealogy,
degree, career and appearance.
Meet lovers with deep consciousness
who are not intimidated by poverty.

The colder and hungrier night becomes,
the more warmly make love.
The deeper your love
the more tears.
Give birth, sisters,
thousands and millions of babies.
Raise them as children with deep consciousness
and let them know your hot tears.

Give birth, sisters.
Multiply them in this history
until they grow up with boiling and overflowing love,
then become a shining revolution.[23]

This male worker dreams about a workers' revolution. In order to achieve the revolution, he wants his sisters to produce many babies who can be revolutionary fighters in the future. He considers his sisters baby machines. He defines women's role in the new society and revolution according to his convenience. He does not ask his sisters what they want from the revolution or how they want to participate in the revolution. He simply gives the orders. His style of telling his wish to his sisters is one of command. It is one-sided. There is no space for women to respond to his command in his poem. Women as subjects of their own lives are silent in his poem.

In actual revolutionary situations women have not been simply baby machines. They have done everything men have done. They have risked their lives like men and been interrogated, tortured, and imprisoned. They have fought in revolutionary battles alongside their male comrades as full human beings and not as baby machines. Leftist men's demands that women be baby machines for their revolution are transcultural; there are many examples of this misguided claim in various parts of the world. Asian women want genuine mutuality with Asian men. We want communities where women and men can participate with their full humanity. When men consider us only as a means of *their* revolution, they are the cause of the breakdown of community, and not we who claim our right to be subjects of our own history.

Q. *If "Asian feminism" is to be in harmony with noble Asian culture, should it not be non-confrontational?*

A. Some Asian feminists do not like the term "Asian feminism," which is used by many Asian men and some Asian women. The reason comes from its usage in the concrete Asian contexts. A group of Korean women sociologists wrote about their response to the frequent use of the term Asian feminism.

It seems to imply that feminism in Asia is different from feminism in the West, that Asian women should be "docile," "polite," and "patient." According to some anti-feminists, women can be liberated as long as they don't deny that their chief role is to be a "good mother" and a "good wife." Supposedly, the "Asian" way should be different from that of the "West." Hence, we should carry on our movement in a non-confronting way.[24]

Asian men are in no position to define what it means to be an Asian woman. There is a clear double standard when men use the word Asian for themselves and for women. When Asian men fight against the Europeanization or the Americanization of their culture due to colonialism and neo-colonialism, they are very confrontational. They are also very militant in their words and deeds and in their struggle for justice under military dictatorships. They are not docile, polite, and patient. Nor are they good citizens as defined by their colonizers or their dictators.

When Asian men use the word *Asian* in their fight against their oppressors, it means being proud subjects of their own history, dignity in struggle, and a determined refusal to accept any kind of colonialism. However, the meaning of being Asian is radically changed when Asian men apply it to women. Asian women, they say, should be the main carriers of traditional Asian culture, a culture mainly defined by the men in power. We should not be aggressive or militant "like Western women" because we Asian women have a noble culture which stretches back many thousands of years. Asian men talk about the importance of harmony and complementarity in Asian culture. They emphasize the beauty of yin and yang and harmony between femininity and masculinity in the Asian community. Any noise and militant actions from Asian women which seem aggressive toward Asian men are automatically dismissed as being non-Asian. It seems the term *Asian* is used most progressively when men use it for themselves but most anachronistically when they apply it to women.[25]

There are two major reasons for this double standard. One is an emphasis on a misguided view of nationalism, and the other is an internalized "orientalism,"[26] which is the product of colonialism. Even though nationalism has been a most important ideology in the fight against colonialism in many parts of Asia, it has also had the tendency to maintain the traditional patriarchal culture at the expense of Asian women. Agitation from women for their rights has been too easily condemned as inappropriate by men in many nationalist struggles. When male nationalists emphasize slogans like *Go back to our own traditions* or *Protect our own culture against colonial culture*, they use *our culture* and *our tradition* without much specification. Every culture has both liberative and oppressive dimensions within its own tradition. When we women look at *our culture* and *our tradition*, we feel its suffocating patriarchal aspects. Therefore, we women find oppressive the indiscriminate emphasis on traditional culture by men in some nationalist movements; for example, Iranian nationalists fought against American imperialism yet forced Iranian women to wear veils again in the name of protecting their cultural heritage.

Asian women also see Asian men's internalized orientalism when Asian men tell them that their liberation struggle must be non-confrontational. Orientalism is the product of Western colonialism. Western colonizers portrayed the Asian as "the other," not fully "advanced" like people in the West. Western colonizers did not want to encounter Asians as people by whom they could be challenged, influenced, and transformed. Westerners objectified Asians without any willingness to meet and learn from them. They called Asians exotic, mysterious, and emotional. Asian men resent Westerners' use of these racial slurs. They reject Westerners' definition of the so-called natural Asian character. However, Asian men seem to have the same attitude as the Western colonizers when they define Asian women's character. Asian men objectify Asian women as "the other," very different from them. Asian men should remember that their attitude toward Asian women reinforces stereotypical images of Asian women which world capitalism exploits. Since so-called gentle and polite and "non-confronting" Asian women seem like the last paradise left in Western men's eyes, they come to Asia to meet "real feminine women" who are not corrupted by the confrontational and militant Western feminist movement. Asian men's emphasis on the non-confrontational Asian woman feeds the sexual fantasies of Western men and contributes to making Asian women into the prostitutes of the world. Listen to this sexual fantasy of a Western man who wrote a book on how to explore Asian women. In *Bangkok's Backstreets: A Guide to the Pleasures of the World's Most Open City*, Bob Todd proudly shares his experiences of how to explore Thai women in detail:

Remember, it doesn't matter if you're overweight, oversexed, and over-the-hill age-wise: to ten million Thai girls you're the ticket to an exciting life of riches and opportunity she can experience no other way. You're doing the girl a favour. . . . By all means, if marriage is on your mind, come and look and learn and sample some inscrutable Oriental yentil to your heart's content.[27]

If Asian men want Asian women to be comrades for the nationalist struggle, they must encourage us to be militant warriors. They should stop giving us the double message to be docile, polite, and non-confrontational to them but militant and confrontational to Western colonizers. We Asian women are not robots Asian men switch on and off according to their convenience. We are persons of integrity. We refuse both Western colonialism and Asian male colonialism of our sexuality and our cultural and social identity.

Q. Feminism is an important liberation movement. However, we have more important movements to deal with in our respective communities such as class struggle, racial struggle, and anti-colonial struggle. Therefore, women should wait until these liberation struggles are complete.

A. This group of people always says they are supporting the feminist movement in their community. However, they add the comment that this is not the right time for their community as a whole to spend energy for woman's liberation. They have other "major" conflicts to solve. We women never seem to have "the right time" for liberation under patriarchal history! If *now* is not the right time for us, we will not have any right time in the future. Many revolutions have promised equal power for women. Yet our concrete historical experience shows that those promises have never been fulfilled after the revolution to the degree women have wanted. We are beginning to recognize that we cannot allow men to be the sole determiners of priority in the freedom struggle. Women cannot wait until the male-defined "major" conflict or "priority" is taken care of. Who, after all, should define the major conflict or priority in the revolutionary struggle? Are not poor women the majority of the population? Are not poor women and children the oppressed among the oppressed in any struggle? If men include the rights of women in the fight for justice, what will they lose in the final liberation? They will not lose anything except their distorted privilege as the male oppressor. If a group wants to have total liberation without letting go of its own privilege guaranteed by the exploitive system, it does not know the fundamental meaning of liberation.

Actually, when men incorporate women's claim for liberation as an intrinsic part of the struggle for total liberation, they accelerate the liberation process. Only when women feel ourselves as full human beings in our own power and responsibility can we use our full potential in the process of liberation. Nobody wants to fight and die for other people's revolution while they remain the slaves of the people they are fighting for. If men get the most benefit from the liberation process at the expense of women's sacrifice, women will not participate in the struggle with all of their being. When women truly know and feel that the struggle will liberate them from bondage, as much as it will liberate men, women will risk their lives for the struggle as much as men will. To prioritize other elements of the struggle by putting women's claims aside is a wrongheaded approach to the total liberation process.

In sum, the question of whether democracy or women's liberation comes first is the wrong question. Asian women cannot set aside their liberation as women and struggle for democracy or against classism and racism as if the liberation process can be chopped up into different pieces. Liberation must be conceived holistically, and no one's experience reveals that fact more than women's. A comment by a black woman in the United States made the same point regarding black women's struggle against sexism in their community:

> Many Black men in the Black liberation movement ask us whether we are "Black first" or "women first." We are very angry about that question because the question presupposes that we women can be compartmentalized like a machine. We are "Black women." We can not be Black from Monday to Thursday, then be women Friday to Sunday. We are Black women for seven days a week. We have Black skin and female genitals at the same time. We can not give up on one for the other. We are Black women all the time.[28]

Like black women, we are Asian women all the time. We cannot compartmentalize aspects of our struggle. Our struggle is a struggle for wholeness. What Asian women want from Asian men is not their "generous understanding" on the "women's problem" but their repentance, a genuine commitment to end their oppression over Asian women, a *metanoia* defined by concrete change. The male oppression of women is not a women's problem. It is a man's problem Asian men have to come to terms with. Only when Asian men in the liberation movement incorporate the liberation of women as an intrinsic ingredient for Asia's struggle for full humanity can their claim for people's liberation have integrity. This means Asian men's support for Asian women's liberation must go beyond tokenism. The Asian women's challenge also means Asian men must transform the way they relate to women, the way they produce and reproduce the world, and the content of their work and world view.

Asian women's theology is being made by women in Asian churches who realize that they cannot continue to accept the place for them defined by Asian men. With other religious and secular sisters, we are determined to create a theology, church, and society that are liberating for women.

3

STRUGGLE TO BE THE SUN AGAIN: ASIAN WOMEN'S THEOLOGICAL REFLECTIONS ON HUMANITY

Prelude

First female voice
1. On my birth there was no singing
   But sadness filled the air;
   No people came to visit
   To bless, or give child-care.
   "Kill her, kill her, kill her,"
   Was what my father said:
   A world-wide declaration
   Because I was a girl.

Male voice
   You are a girl, a misery;
   You'll eat me out, you're drudgery!

Chorus
Female voices
   My mother wept in silence
   As only mothers do;
   Pitying my misfortune
   That she had suffered too.

2. I grew up like my brothers,
   With body, mind and soul,
   Yet my head was never schooled.
   My body—my body was fully used.
   I worked at home and outside
   And weary dared not feel.
   I offered food and comfort
   When the men returned from field.

36

Male voice

House and housework is your good
fortune.
Keep your place, before I'm too
violent!

Chorus
Female voices

My mother shared my discomfort
As only mothers do;
Pitying my misfortune
For she was suffering too.

3. My youth was my disaster
   And not the prime of life —
   For lo! I had to marry
   And slave as someone's wife.
   My spirit wants an answer for my
   unequal place,
   The indignities you offer
   After companionable embrace.

Male voice

Man is God, God is Man.
You are a woman, woman, woman!

Chorus

My mother knew my anguish
As only mothers do;
pitying my misfortune
For she had lived it too.

4. And now I am a widow,
   Insignificant, weak and old.
   I wonder on my death-day
   Will tears or relief hold sway?
   It was a sad beginning,
   It appears a lonely ending.
   And my only solace, the Holy Book,
   Makes me fully sinful look.

Male voice

In the name of your father, your
husband
and your son,
Be obedient, be respectful, be
grateful,
hold your peace!

Chorus
Female voices

My daughter feels my sorrow
As only daughters do;
Angry at my misfortunes
And she wants to break it through.

Second female voice	5. I will break these many bondages I'll release myself from shame; I will learn, I will teach all womankind Freedom from disdain. God created woman and man In God's very own image By the power of God, the woman is blessed In my birth, life and death, *I am blessed*.
Male voices	Truly you are a *woman* honoured by God, by us; Partner in our striving Towards all human rights.
Chorus Female voices	All women join together In solidarity against oppression, And together help our fellow-men Develop this earth and humans.[1]

What does it mean to be fully human? This is the question Asian women ask when they encounter overwhelming suffering and injustice in their lives. Asian women ask hard questions about the meaning of humanity and God because they are hurt. They want to find meaning in their seemingly meaningless suffering in order to survive as human beings with dignity and integrity. From birth to death Asian women have to fight against "death-wishes" from male-dominated society. In fact, this curse against Asian women begins even before their biological conception. Asian parents pray to the gods and goddesses asking for the conception of a son. Once conception has occurred, they hope for a son throughout the pregnancy. Upon the birth of a daughter, many Asian parents are greatly disappointed. Some Korean women are named Sup-sup-ie, which means regrettable or disappointing. Others are called Keun-nae-mi, which means terminating (the birth of the next daughter). Many Asian women arrive in this men-worshiping, women-despising world only to receive "curse-full" names. Some are destroyed in their mother's womb after amniocentesis[2] or right after birth by the hands of family members who wanted a son. Female children generally are more poorly fed, less educated and overworked when compared with male children. Even after they grow up, women's lives only get worse under oppressive public and domestic structures based on classism, racism, sexism, castism, and cultural imperialism. Their bodies are controlled and their labors are exploited.[3]

Asian women's self-understanding grows out of this brutal reality. When I was growing up in Korea, my mother and aunts often said to me, "If you

start to ask the meaning of pain and suffering, you begin to know God."
Pain and suffering, therefore, are the epistemological starting point for
Asian women in their search for the meaning of full humanity. The Asian
woman knows the depth of humanity and the aching hearts of other women
because she has suffered and she has lived in pain. This knowing is different
from that of the privileged men who are the cause of Asian women's pain
and suffering. Asian women's epistemology is an *epistemology from the broken body*, a broken body longing for healing and wholeness.

In their brokenness and longing for a full humanity, Asian women have
met and come to know God. What then is the meaning of knowing God?
For Asian women it means to understand the ultimate purpose of their
lives and to discover the meaning of existence in this history and cosmos.
Asian women are extremely religious since their lives are characterized with
much suffering and pain. Asian women's understanding of humanity is
directly related with their understanding of who God is and what God does
in the midst of their suffering and their struggle for liberation.

What does it mean to be fully human for Asian women when their bodies
are beaten, torn, choked, burnt, and dismembered? Asian women have
reflected on this hard question out of their broken-body experiences,
searching for ways to survive as human beings with a sense of self-worth
and purpose. Privately and publicly, both as victims of oppression and as
agents of liberation, they have expressed their survival wisdom from the
underside of patriarchal history through poems, songs, and stories. Asian
women know they cannot endure meaningless suffering if they do not dream
of a world defined by wholeness, justice, and peace. They also know they
will perish without a vision of life in its fullness and in its deepest beauty.
The following theological reflections of Asian women on the meaning of
suffering, evil, sin, and God's image are not the product of abstract metaphysical reflections on so-called human nature as found in dominant Western and Eastern theologies and philosophies. Rather, they are remedies
and medicines for the healing of broken bodies and wounded spirits from
many "wounded healers" in Asia. Let us listen to the stories of Asian
women.

To Be Human Is To Suffer and Resist

Asian women cannot define humanity apart from their suffering. To be
human for Asian women is to suffer because suffering is the major element
of their life experiences. Therefore, Asian women must come to terms with
their suffering in order to understand who they are as human beings.

Asian women have become "no-body" under the body-killing structures
of the powers and the principalities of this world, such as foreign domination, state repression, militarism, racial strife, and capitalism. The systematic women-hate under patriarchal society makes Asian women's lives

miserable. Asian women who attended the EATWOT Asian women's conference described this sinful situation of oppression:

> In all spheres of Asian society, women are dominated, dehumanized, and de-womanized; they are discriminated against, exploited, harassed, sexually used, abused, and viewed as inferior beings who must always subordinate themselves to the so-called male supremacy. In the home, church, law, education, and media, women have been treated with bias and condescension. In Asia and all over the world, the myth of subservient, servile Asian women is blatantly peddled to reinforce the dominant male sterotype image.[4]

The experience of the many forms of oppression in Asian women's lives leads them to ask what the cause is of all the evil around them. They think the evil arises from human sin. But they differentiate the oppressors' sin from that of the oppressed. For Asian women, the oppressors' sin lies in their "lust for power, prestige, knowledge, and wealth."[5] The oppressors' "greed" and their "desire to dominate the other" are "the basis of class/patriarchal society."[6] These characteristics lead people to "the distortion of the self/other relationship" and "domination and control."[7] Human sin is not just a personal attitude. It has "collective" and "systemic" character.[8] Human sin, then, is manifested through colonialism, neo-colonialism, capitalism, racism, classism, castism, and sexism.

While Asian women are angered by the sin of the oppressors, they also acknowledge the sin of the oppressed. This includes internalized self-hate, horizontal violence, and ignorance. Internalized self-hate, caused by many forms of colonialism and patriarchy, makes them distrust themselves and other women. Asian women confess that they lack "self-confidence" and are "unwilling to encourage other women" to aspire to leadership positions.[9] In many cases they direct their anger of oppression not at the oppressor but at each other. This leads to "horizontal violence" among women.[10]

The liturgy used at the Indian Women Theologians' Conference held at Bangalore, India, November 1984, expresses Asian women's understanding of sin under patriarchal society:[11]

Leader-1:	We know ourselves to be a people who distort sexuality.
All:	We are separated from ourselves, each other, and the God of life.
Leader-2:	Let us confess our brokenness.
Women:	As women caught in our tradition, we confess that we have helped perpetuate the myth of feminine inferiority by adopting the role of natural followers.

Men:	As men caught in our tradition, we confess that we have helped perpetuate the myth of masculine superiority by assuming the role of natural leaders.
Women:	As women, we confess that we have been willing to limit our image to that of wives, mothers, and sexual objects for men.
Men:	As men, we confess that we have often seen women as sexual objects. We have been a part of restricting their roles to those of wives and mothers.
Women:	We confess that we have not sought our own real identity in Scripture and history. We have failed to trust ourselves and other women. We have been our own worst enemies.
Men:	We confess that we have perpetuated religious teachings which reinforce illusions of male supremacy. While we exhalt servanthood, we leave the menial tasks to women.
Women:	We confess that we have participated in a system which inhibits and denies self-affirmation and creativity to all sorts and conditions of persons.
Men:	We confess that we have paid lip service to universal equality, yet our lives are based on sexual discrimination and, in fact, we have placed women in subordinate positions.
All:	Moved by the power of Holy Spirit, we accuse ourselves because we have not allowed God to form us as a new people. We confess our sin to God, to the Church and to the World. We pledge to work for reconciliation with one another.
Leader-1:	In the name of our creator, our redeemer, our comforter, you are forgiven. You are freed from the past and its oppression. You are free to move to a new future of mutuality and love, taking into account the sins of the past and not bound by them. The Gift is complete; live in the grace of God's love.[12]

As mentioned in the above liturgy, oppression makes the oppressed experience separation of self. The oppressed woman experiences a most severe split within herself. The sense of who she wants to be as a human being and her reality of who she is in capitalist/patriarchal society are radically different and opposite, and this situation produces shame, guilt, and self-hate. Continuous, prolonged shame, guilt, and self-hate then lead Asian women to the pseudo-safety of non-feeling. Numbing oneself for survival is the most tragic stage for the oppressed because the individual loses the power to resist. Through the process of numbing, individuals become separated from themselves, each other, and the God of Life. Asian women call this numbing the separation sin. Even though this separation is caused by the oppression of capitalist/patriarchal society, Asian women do not think they are sin-free. Asian women accept their full responsibility for perpetuating oppression by merely obeying the oppressor and failing to trust themselves and other women.

Korean women theologians, along with Korean male minjung[13] theologians, have articulated another mode of responding to the sinful situation of the oppressed. They call it *han*. *Han* is the most prevalent feeling among Korean people, who have been violated throughout their history by the surrounding powerful countries. This feeling arises from a sense of impasse. Often Korean people, especially the poor and women, have not had any access to public channels through which they can challenge the injustices done to them. They have long been silenced by physical and psychological intimidation and actual bodily violence by the oppressor. When there is no place where they can express their true selves, their true feelings, the oppressed become "stuck" inside. This unexpressed anger and resentment stemming from social powerlessness forms a "lump" in their spirit. This lump often leads to a lump in the body, by which I mean the oppressed often disintegrate bodily as well as psychologically.

Korean minjung theologian Hyun Young Hak has explored the feeling of *han* further:

> *Han* is a sense of unresolved resentment against injustice suffered, a sense of helplessness because of the overwhelming odds against, a feeling of total abandonment ("Why has Thou forsaken Me"), a feeling of acute pain and sorrow in one's guts and bowels making the whole body writhe and wiggle, and an obstinate urge to take "revenge" and to right the wrong all these constitute.[14]

Both Korean women theologians and Korean male minjung theologians agree that oppressed Korean women's core experiences in recent Korean history have been *han*. Oppressed Korean women are the "minjung within the minjung" and the "*han* of the *han*."

Korean women's way of dealing with *han* throughout their painful history could offer some precious survival resources for other Asian women and oppressed people from many backgrounds. There are two modes of dealing with *han* among Korean women. One is accepting it, and the other is refusing it. The passive acceptance of *han* can be defined as resignation. Koreans call this aspect "*jung han*."[15] Many Asian religio-cultural traditions support this attitude. Buddhism and Hinduism see human life as suffering; to suffer means to be a normal human being. The teachings of fate make people think that what happens in their lives is something they deserve. Since their lives are predetermined, nothing can be done to change things. The only option they have is to be at peace with their situation and live out a dutiful life for the reward of better fate in the next life. Korean women have expressed the sadness of their fate through their songs, poems, and dances. In this cultural atmosphere, the introduction of a rigid doctrine of predestination and the cross by fundamentalist Western missionaries added more burden to Korean Christian women's lives. It made them more passive and accepting of their own victimization. To be a Christian was interpreted in such a way that women were encouraged to suffer peacefully, the way Jesus suffered on the cross, because it was God's will, predestined in eternity.

The passive acceptance, however, of Korean women's fate is not the full story of Korean women's lives. Korean women are also fighters who refuse to accept their *han*-ridden lives. They are angry about their situation and seek revenge or revolutionary change. Koreans call this aspect *won-han*.[16] Throughout history Korean women have untangled their complex webs of *han* through their survival wisdom. In the Korean tradition the untanglement of *han* is named *han-pu-ri*. Gentle ways of *han-pu-ri* have been through songs, dances, and rituals; and militant ways of *han-pu-ri* have been developed by farmers, workers, slum dwellers, and women's organized political movements.

Recently Korean women theologians have devoted much of their energy and time to rediscovering women's survival resources in their own tradition. Lee Oo Chung, a professor of New Testament studies whose political activism with the people's movement led to her losing her position under government coercion, was concerned with Korean women's suffering and resistance as expressed in traditional Korean songs, proverbs, folk songs, and myths.[17] According to Lee, Korean women have been not only passive victims, who have been frustrated by overwhelming injustices in the world and have accepted their oppression, they have also been the active agents of liberation. Korean women, Lee contends, have established critical positions through humor and satire "which have enabled them to go beyond their paralysing sadness."[18] Through folktales and songs Korean women have satirized the greed of political authorities, the foolishness of aristocrats and intellectuals, the hypocrisy of male priests and their religious institutions, and the brutality of the patriarchal family. Lee believes that the life-giving power of the survival wisdom of Korean minjung women, who have endured all the absurdities and violence directed against them, could lead many Third World people to overcome the despair of militarism, nuclear war, and the destruction of nature.

In her analysis of Korean women's wisdom, Lee names three treasures she calls "present centered optimism," "the conviction in one's work," and "the love for neighbours."[19] Lee finds Korean folklore, myth, and songs free of the heroic despair found in those of the West. She does not see in this Korean folk tradition any dualism between body and spirit or between the secular world and the spiritual world. Korean women believe that they will eventually *win their victory in this world* if they endure and fight together. It is this belief Lee calls present centered optimism. She also emphasizes the joy of work and deep conviction in one's work as found in traditional Korean labor songs, which enabled Korean minjung women to celebrate life in harmony with nature. For minjung women nature is the ground of life and the breast of Mother Earth; being in touch with and working with nature is both precious and joyful. Lee observes that this attitude toward work can be found in many Korean folk arts.

Another important resource for women's survival is their love for neighbors. Lee contends that in Korean folklore and myth, Korean women overcome evil not by violence but by a wisdom based on love of neighbors. She demonstrates how male gods are portrayed as greedy flesh eaters who eat their neighbors' food and otherwise violate people. Female goddesses, on the other hand, are portrayed as agricultural workers who work diligently and gather grains and fruits from the earth while protecting, not violating, humans.[20]

If the above examples show women's resistance of *han* in gentle ways, Korean women in recent history have also used militant resistance. The most militant workers' movement and slum dwellers' movement have been led by women. Women are the scapegoats of rapid economic development in Korea. Their fight for "survival rights" has been intense and persistent. Currently, women's movements against capitalism and patriarchal society are flourishing in Korea and many Asian countries. There are the movements against dowry and sati in India; the movements against military dictatorships, multinational corporations, and the international prostitution industry in the Philippines; the ecological movement in Japan; and the movement against state terrorism in Sri Lanka. Asian women have discovered their true selves and have become stronger through their participation in these movements.[21]

Sister Sigrid of India observes three steps women take when they are transformed from oppressed victims to agents of liberation. She names them as "appreciation—education—association."[22] According to Sigrid, women begin to be transformed when they start to appreciate their personhood. Then women need to train themselves in order to equip themselves as effective agents of liberation. Finally, women need to join a larger community of women to sustain their power and make social change possible. These three steps are not chronologically sequential, but are three different aspects of women's transformation.

Other Asian women propose similar ideas about the women's liberation process. Most women think self-awakening/self-affirmation is the first step toward growth and liberation.[23] Women achieve self-awakening and self-affirmation through critical reflection and creativity. If critical reflection enables them to see the oppressive power of the false self imposed upon them by patriarchal society, women's creativity enables them to discover their true self. Indian feminist artist Lucy D'Souza shares the meaning of creativity in her life:

> To me creativity means discovering and coming to terms with myself, by understanding and accepting myself. This also helps me to accept others as they are and to build up the society in which we live.[24]

Self-awakened/self-affirming women take a stand and change their personal and political relationships. On the personal level women define new relationships with the men in their lives. Such women are "unwilling to stand in awe of them [men] or be pushed around, manipulated, or dominated."[25] Many Asian women witness how their marriages have been changed after their self-awakening/self-affirmation as women with full humanity. One Filipino peasant woman who started to break out from the old religious and cultural teachings about what women should be through attending a Bible study group in her basic Christian community, shares the changes in her marriage:

> We obeyed our husbands in fear and trembling; they were the men, the bread winners. . . . Before, our irate husbands would say, "Why don't you wear the pants?" But now what is right is followed, we are equals. We have awakened and have stopped saying yes and yes. This we have learned from Bible study—freedom and equal rights.[26]

Some women make a radical break with patriarchal marriage through divorce, which is scandalous in Asia. Most divorced women in Asia are ostracized and become a target for the majority's anger and fear. For a divorced woman to attend a marriage ceremony is discouraged in many Asian countries because the divorced woman's presence is considered inauspicious. One Indian woman expresses her struggles and blessings as a divorced woman eloquently:

> I married early and this personhood was the first position of destruction and attack. Then and before, my preservation took place in writing poetry and expressing myself in song. This became the only means of inner survival. . . . I emerged as a "woman" only when I chose to be free of bondage in marriage. With that choice I became a woman—disrespected, discriminated against, redundant. Then I became a woman—fighting to live, to retain my humanity. I chose to become myself again. My struggle to become a "woman" is a struggle to personhood—to become human.[27]

Other women choose lesbianism in order to protect and heal themselves from male violence. Lesbianism is a taboo in Asian society, not to be talked about in public places. Most Asians think of homosexuality as a Western issue, not an Eastern one. Yet the international sex tourism and prostitution industry, which were initiated by First World men's greed and interventionist foreign and military policies in Asia, have made many parts of Asia into brothels. Many poor Asian women in the Philippines, Thailand, Korea, and other countries have been violated by the men from the First World and also by men from their own countries. Asian women's bodies are literally torn, choked, bruised, and killed by men. A prostitute in Korea shared her feelings about men in her support group with other Korean women who wanted to build solidarity with her.[28] She felt much shame and guilt about the selling of her body even though it was the only option she had for survival. She also felt strong anger toward all men:

> All men are the same when they take off their pants. They are all animals. It does not matter whether they are rich or poor, highly educated or ignorant. . . . My customers' jobs vary. Some of them are businessmen, a professor, a politician and even a minister. But what they do to me is all the same. They only think how to use me most for their pleasure.[29]

This anger towards men can be found in many women's writings on prostitution from different Asian countries. Lesbianism among prostitutes has become a visible phenomenon in the Philippines, one of the Asian countries most sexually exploited by the First World because of the military bases of the United States. When theologically trained women of the Philippines joined together for a consultation, they had a serious discussion on homosexuality.[30] One participant raised the issue of homosexuality and its biblical implication because "homosexuality is becoming a part of our culture."[31] A Filipino biblical scholar, Elizabeth G. Dominguez, responded to this question by quoting two Bible verses. One came from 2 Samuel 1 and the other was from Ruth 1:16ff. Dominguez pointed out that in David's song for Jonathan, David confesses that Jonathan's love to him was "wonderful, passing the love of a woman." Dominguez also points out that love between Ruth and Naomi is "unreserved sharing of love." She contends:

> If homosexuality has to be condemned, it has to be condemned only on the grounds that persons are degraded. . . . If homosexuality prevails in our society, perhaps it is because heterosexual relationships are being exhausted because of the kind of society we are in, no longer being able to give human caring that human beings need. I would like to raise this question because what is basic is human caring that is experienced by both individuals so that their humanity is held.[32]

If Asian women's changing relationships with their primary partners is a sign of self-awakened and self-affirming women in their personal lives, then the organized women's movement in solidarity with the larger people's movement for justice is a sign of Asian women's self-love in public life. Women all over Asia have organized for political change. Korean women refuse to pay the fee for government-owned television because it portrays a degrading image of women in its programs and deceives people for the benefit of the military government. Filipino deaconesses walked out of their Methodist Annual Conference because the hierarchy did not give them voting rights. Japanese women demonstrated against Japan's reviving emperor worship and militarism, which perpetuates women's oppression. Indian women have marched and had hunger strikes to abolish the personal and religious laws which violate Indian women's civil rights.[33] Women are rising up all over Asia! They have awakened from centuries-old sleep and now move mountains. The prophecy by our Asian foremothers has come true in our generation. Their vision for the future inspires us in our continuous journey for freedom:

> The mountain-moving day is coming.
> I say so, yet others doubt.
> Only awhile the mountain sleeps.
> In the past
> All mountains moved in fire,
> Yet you may not believe it.
> Oh man, this alone believe,
> All sleeping women now will awake and move.[34]

To Be Human Is To Be Created in God's Image

In their search for full humanity, Asian women receive strength through biblical teachings. However, for Asian women good news from the Bible is not a free gift to accept without suspicion since the Bible carries so many oppressive messages for women.

Out of many contradictory teachings in the Bible, Asian women use most frequently the teaching from Genesis which contains the message that men and women are created equally in God's image (Gen. 1:27,28). *In God's Image* is an important biblical phrase Asian women have adopted to define their perspectives on humanity. Human beings—men and women—were created in God's image. Who we are as humans is defined by who God is. This may appear to be quite Barthian or neo-orthodox, and perhaps that influence has affected Asian women's language, but the key to their anthropology is really not theology. It is in fact the other way around. The key to their theology is anthropology, that is, Asian women's experience of suffering and hope. God is defined by their experience. To understand Asian women's perspectives on humanity, therefore, it is important to note a transformation in their thinking about God.

God as Both Female and Male

Many Asian women think God has both female and male qualities in the God-self. It is natural for Asian women to think of the Godhead as male and female because there are many male gods and female goddesses in Asian religious cultures. Padma Gallup from India claims that Western Christianity lost the inclusive quality of the Godhead who has both male and female sides because it was "wrapped in layers of ponderous patriarchy, Zoroastrian dualism, Greek philosophy, and the ethics of the marketplace and morality of the dominant male of the Puritan tradition."[35] Gallup also proposes that Asian feminist theology should draw its sources from "its own millenia-old culture, and all the living faiths of its neighbors."[36] She gains insights from Hindu religion and culture in order to understand *Imago Dei* from an Asian women's perspective. For Gallup, the Hindu image of *Arthanaressvara* (the deity in which the masculine *Sivam* [absolute good or love] and the feminine *Sakti* [absolute power] form a whole in which neither can function without the other) is a positive model for the *Imago Dei* for Asian women. Gallup thinks that "a concept of the Godhead that holds the masculine and feminine in equivalence could possibly engender non-dualistic, non-competitive modes of thought and action."[37]

Many Asian women believe that an inclusive image of God who has both male and female sides promotes equality and harmony between men and women: a "partnership of equals."[38] However, they also are concerned about the way harmony and complementarity are used against women in Asia. Virginia Fabella warns Asian women that the emphasis on complementarity and harmony should not be achieved at the expense of women's equality. She explains how many Asian churches are using complementarity for men's convenience in order to perpetuate stereotypical feminine roles for women. Fabella claims that for liberated women, "complementarity is acceptable only if it respects equality."[39] In sum, Asian women's yearning for and rediscovery of a Godhead which contains both male and female qualities is the same yearning for full humanity in which both males and females are fully respected as equal partners.

God as Community

Asian women view God not as an individual but as a community. When she interprets Genesis 1:26, Elizabeth Dominguez from the Philippines claims: "To be in the image of God is to be in community. It is not simply a man or a woman who can reflect God, but it is the community in relationship."[40] In a genuine community everyone is a "steward" to one another. "All the parts are for one another and all the parts have their role."[41] This community is characterized by "interdependence," "harmony," and "mutual growth."[42]

The image of God as "the community in relationship" empowers Asian women to get out of their individualism. It also encourages them to honor their responsibility and rights as a part of the community. Interdependence, harmony, and mutual growth are impossible when there is no balance of power. Monopolized power destroys community by destroying mutuality. Therefore, in this image of God as the community in relationship, there is no place for only one, solitary, all-powerful God who sits on the top of the hierarchical power pyramid and dominates all other living beings. Where there is no mutual relationship, there is no human experience of God. Asian women emphasize the importance of community in their theologies because only in community can humanity reflect God and fulfill the image of God in which we were created for mutual relationship.

God as Creator in Nature and in History

Asian women believe God is also "creator of this beautiful universe in all its splendour and variety."[43] They experience this creator God in their own "creativity as a woman who gives birth, as a cook, gardener, communicator, as a writer, as a creator of the environment, atmosphere, life."[44] The creator God draws people out of their own captivity and invites them to be a co-creator with God. When Asian women touch their own creativity and create their own healing, they touch the life source—God. They create babies, food, and gardens. They also create history. God is not a prime mover who just started the universe and then sat back out of the universe after creation. God's creation is a continuous, ongoing process. This creator God walks with us in our own creation of history. This is the "God of history who is with the oppressed people in their struggle for justice."[45]

When women get out of their oppression and create alternative structures which are life-giving for them, they meet their God through the process of liberation. They know the God of history takes sides with the oppressed as witnessed in Exodus, Jesus' life, and the many unbeatable people's movements in Asia. With their trust in this God, Asian women draw strength for their struggle for justice. In their faith, Asian women know they are invited as God's partner to the covenant of "justice, peace and the integrity of creation."[46]

God as Life-Giving Spirit

The emerging generation of Asian women theologians emphasize God as a life-giving spirit they can encounter *within* themselves and *in* everything which fosters life. This move is the manifesto of their shift in the theological paradigm, which is different from that of the older generation. Until recently, Asian theologies have been heavily based on the neo-orthodox theology from the West. Neo-orthodox theology promotes a transcendent, absolute other God, and Christian revelatory truth over other religious truth. The younger generation of Asian women theologians lift up the immanence of God in their theologies. They are longing for an image of God which is all-embracing: God as life-giving spirit who is present everywhere and moves everywhere opens the door for a new understanding of the divine. Indian dancer/musican/poet Susan Joseph confesses that her image of the spirit is a bird. She says:

> The holy spirit was my bird. My encounter with the Spirit moved my image of God into a more inclusive, unrestrictive image.[47]

Lee Sun Ai resonates with this inclusive, unrestrictive image of God, when she writes:

> God is movement
> God is the angry surf
> God is like mother
> God is like father
> God is like friends
> God is power of being
> God is power of living
> God is power of giving birth[48]

When women see God as an all-inclusive reality in everything (especially within themselves), they begin to trust their personal power. Astrid Lobo, an Indian scientist and active lay leader in the Catholic church, confesses that her growing confidence in herself as a human person is directly related to her new image of God. She contends:

> As a woman it is important for me that I am in God, and God is in me. No longer do I see God as a rescuer. I see her more as power and strength within me.[49]

While drawing new insights from Hinduism, the universality of God, Lobo discovers God within herself as the "Supreme Center." The more she looks within herself for the source of strength, the more she begins to trust her own power. She stops begging for God to rescue her as a helpless victim. Lobo shares this new understanding further:

> I no longer see the victim-rescuer game as healthy, so I have learnt to shed the needless dependence on God. I am increasingly aware of the resources God has given me. I feel strongly the need to develop and create as my response to God's love shown in my creation.[50]

God as Mother and Woman

Many Asian women think God as a life-giving power can be naturally personified as mother and woman because woman gives birth to her children and her family members by nurturing them. In many Asian women's writings, God is portrayed as mother and woman. Some Asian women claim that women are more sensitive to fostering life than men because of women's experience of giving birth and nurturing others. A group of Asian women emphasized the point by reflecting on the event of Moses' birth and killing of male infants in Exodus:

> Every woman is close to life and loves her child. Woman is life and love. The killing of the male baby is ironic of the two edged sword that patriarchy has in itself, namely, in male power is also death.[51]

God as mother and woman challenges the old concept which emphasized, along with other attributes, God as immutable and unchangeable. Woman's body grows and changes radically through menstruation and pregnancy compared to the male body. God as mother is more approachable and personable. When Asian women begin to imagine God as woman and mother, they also begin to accept their own bodies and their own womanhood in its fullness. The female God accepts us as we are more than the patriarchal male God. This female God is a vulnerable God who is willing to be changed and transformed in her interaction with Asian women in their everyday life experiences. This God is a God who talks to Asian women, listens to their story, and weeps with them. This God is a God who struggles with Asian women in their claims of power in this world, a God who is growing, changing, and walking with them.

Asian women's trust in this God enables them to trust themselves and to hope in the midst of their hopelessness. The power of God evokes in Asian women a different kind of power, which has been lost in patriarchal religion and society:

> The power that fosters life rather than death
> the power of working together,
> the power of experiencing one's true feelings,
> the power of acclaiming others and
> enabling them to realize their full
> potential as human beings.[52]

With this new power Asian women struggle to be persons with power for self-determination. They dream of a new world where woman is not the moon which has to change according to the sun. Rather they want to become the sun who shines in its own light out of its burning core of life, fostering life on the earth.

> Originally, woman was the Sun.
> She was an authentic person.
> But now woman is the moon.
> She lives by depending on another
> and she shines by reflecting

another's light.
Her face has a sickly pallor.

We must now regain our hidden sun.
"Reveal our hidden sun!
Rediscover our natural gifts!"
This is the ceaseless cry
Which forces itself into our hearts;
it is our irrepressible
and unquenchable desire.
It is our final,
complete,
and only instinct
through which
our various
separate instincts
are unified.[53]

In Asian women's perspective, knowledge of self leads to a knowledge of God. In their suffering, Asian women meet God, who in turn discloses that they were created in the divine image, full and equal participants in the community with men. To know the self is to know God for Christian Asian women. Asian women's knowledge of Jesus Christ, who has become a symbol of full humanity, is the subject of the next chapter.

4

WHO IS JESUS
FOR ASIAN WOMEN?

Traditional Images

In order to express their experiences of Jesus, the majority of Asian women use the traditional titles that they received from missionaries. Since many Christian churches in Asia are still dominated by Western missionary theologies and androcentric interpretations of the Bible, some Asian women's theologies on the surface look similar to Western missionary or Asian male theologies. However, when we look closely at the Asian women's usage of the traditional titles of Jesus, we can find the emergence of new meaning out of the old language. The following are examples of traditional images of Jesus which have gone through the welding of meaning by the experiences of Asian women.

Jesus as Suffering Servant

The most prevailing image of Jesus among Asian women's theological expressions is the image of the suffering servant. Asian Christian women seem to feel most comfortable with this image of Jesus whether they are theologically conservative or progressive.

According to the "Summary Statement from the Theological Study Group of Christology,"[1] developed by the Asian Women's Theological Conference, Singapore, Asian Christian women from many different countries defined Jesus as "the prophetic messiah whose role is that of the suffering servant," the one who "offers himself as ransom for many." They claimed that "through his suffering messiahship, he creates a new humanity."[2]

Asian Christian women at the Singapore conference rejected such images of Jesus as "triumphal King" and "authoritative high priest."[3] They contended that these images of Jesus have "served to support a patriarchal religious consciousness in the Church and in theology."[4] Jesus became the Messiah through his suffering in service to others, not by his domination over others. Like Korean theologian Choi Man Ja, many Asian Christian women make connections between their humanity and Jesus' humanity through "suffering and obedience."[5] Because Asian women's life experience is filled with "suffering and obedience," it seems natural for Asian women to meet Jesus through the experience that is most familiar to them.

When Asian women live through the hardship of suffering and obedience their family, society, and culture inflict upon them, they need a language that can define the meaning of their experience. The image of a suffering Jesus enables Asian women to see meaning in their own suffering. Jesus suffered for others as Asian women suffer for their families and other community members. As Jesus' suffering was salvific, Asian women are beginning to view their own suffering as redemptive. They are making meaning out of their suffering through the stories of Jesus' life and death. As Jesus' suffering for others was life-giving, so Asian women's suffering is being viewed as a source of empowerment for themselves and for others whose experience is defined by oppression.

However, making meaning out of suffering is a dangerous business. It can be both a seed for liberation and an opium for the oppression of Asian women. These two conflicting possibilities shape Asian women's experience of encounter with Jesus.

Asian women have believed in Jesus *in spite of* many contradictory experiences they receive from their families, churches, and societies. Believing *in spite of* great contradictions is the only option for many Asian women who are seeking to be Christian. For example, their fathers are supposed to be the protectors, the ones who give Asian women safety in an oppressive world, providing food, shelter, and clothing. But too often Asian women are beaten by their fathers or sold into child marriage or prostitution. Asian women's husbands are supposed to love them, but frequently they batter their wives in the name of love and family harmony. Asian women's brothers are supposed to support and encourage them, but they instead often further their own higher educations by tacitly using their Asian sisters, ignoring the reality that their sisters are selling their bodies to pay for tuition. The promises of safety, love, and nurturing have not been fulfilled. Asian women have trusted their beloved men, but their men have often betrayed them. Yet Asian women still hope, still believe that, "Maybe someday, somewhere, somebody will love me and nurture me as I am." Is Jesus that somebody?

Some Asian women have found Jesus as the one who really loves and respects them as human beings with dignity, while the other men in their lives have betrayed them. At the Singapore conference, Komol Arayapraatep, a Christian woman from Thailand, shared her appreciation of Jesus:

We women are always very grateful to Jesus the Christ. It is because of him that we can see God's grace for women. God saw to it that women had a vital part in the life of Jesus the Christ from his birth to his death and resurrection.[6]

Yet the church's teachings about Jesus are very similar to what their fathers, husbands, and brothers say to Asian women, rather than what Jesus actually says to them in the gospels. The church tells Asian women:

Be obedient and patient as Jesus was to his heavenly father. He endured suffering and death on the cross. That is what good Christian women are supposed to do. When you go through all the suffering, you too, like Jesus, will have a resurrection someday in heaven. Remember, without the cross, there will be no resurrection; no pain, no gain. You must die first in order to live.[7]

This is a hard and confusing teaching for Asian women. They are asking, "Why should we die in order to gain Jesus' love? Can't we love Jesus while being fully alive?" For Asian women self-denial and love are always applied to women in the church as they are in the family. But why isn't this teaching applied to men?

Western colonialism and neo-colonialism have created an added burden to Asian women's belief in Jesus. When Western Christians brought Jesus to Asia, many also brought with them opium and guns.[8] They taught Asians the love of Jesus while they gave Asians the slow death of opium or the fast death of a bullet. When the soldiers of the United States of America raped Vietnamese women and children and killed many Vietnamese people with Agent Orange, guns, and bombs in the name of democracy, the people of the United States still sang, "God Bless America." Death and love are connected in missionary acts whether they are religious or secular.[9]

Some Asian women still choose Jesus in spite of these contradictory personal and political experiences. Why have they continued to choose Jesus over and over again? Where was Jesus when Asian women's bodies were battered, raped, and burned? What has he done to protect them from suffering? Who is Jesus for Asian women? Is he like his own father, who allowed his son to be killed by Roman colonial power and religious hierarchies even though he cried out for help? ("My God, my God, why have you forsaken me?") Is Jesus like one of those irresponsible, frustrated Asian men who promise their lover and wife love and "the good life" but then, after stealing the woman's heart and body, say: "I will come back soon with money and gifts. While I am away, take care of *my* children and old parents. Be loyal to me." Of course such men almost never come back to their hopelessly waiting lover and wife, leaving all the burdens of survival on her shoulders. Are Asian women stuck in the battered women's vicious cycle of passive dependency? In Jesus are they again choosing a male whom they again try to love in spite of his neglect and abandonment simply because they know of no other type of relationship with men?

Some brave Asian women proclaim a resounding no to this endlessly confusing love game defined by "in spite of." They say they love Jesus *because of* and not *in spite of* who he is. They refuse to accept old, familiar ways of relating to their loved ones, which were based on forced sacrifice by women. Rather, they choose the *respect* of self. Jesus is only good for these Asian women when he affirms, respects, and is actively present with them in their long and hard journey for liberation and wholeness. Asian women are discovering with much passion and compassion that Jesus takes sides with the silenced Asian women in his solidarity with all oppressed people. This Jesus is Asian women's new lover, comrade, and suffering servant.

One example of choosing Jesus *because of* is witnessed by a Filipino, Lydia Lascano, a community organizer for slum dwellers for more than ten years, who presented her experience of Jesus as a suffering servant actively present with Filipino women in their suffering and resistance.[10] She believes Jesus' suffering has two different moments. One is "passive" and the other is "active." She identifies poor Filipino women's suffering under colonialism, military dictatorship, and male domination with the suffering of Jesus. She quotes from Isaiah as an example of the passive moment of Jesus' suffering:

He had no beauty, no majesty to draw our eyes, no grace to make us delight in him; his form, disfigured, lost all the likeness of a man. Without beauty, without majesty . . . a thing despised and rejected by men, a man of sorrows familiar with suffering (Is. 53:2-3 NEB).

Lascano sees that the humiliation and dehumanization of the suffering servant are the same as the core experience of Filipino women. Many Filipino women are "suffering passively without hope of freeing themselves" due to the overwhelming hardship of their day-to-day survival and the unawareness of the root causes of their oppression.[11] The suffering servant image of Jesus expresses well the reality that Filipino women are undergoing.[12] Jesus' passive moment of undergoing suffering is very important for poor Filipino women because they then can trust Jesus for his *lived* suffering. Jesus does not lecture or preach about suffering in the way the institutional church does. He knows women's suffering because he was the one who once suffered helplessly like them.

Lydia Lascano also identifies an active moment of Jesus' suffering which contrasts to the passive moment. The active moment of Jesus' suffering is "doing" and "accompanying" as acts of solidarity. For her, to accompany is to be beside and walk with someone.[13] Jesus is actively present in the Filipino women's struggle for liberation, accompanying them in their doing justice. For Filipino women Jesus is not a dispassionate observer of their struggle. Rather, Jesus is an active participant in their fight for justice. Another Filipino woman, Virginia Fabella, explains this accompanying and doing aspect of Jesus' suffering in this way: "Because he stood for all he taught and did, he consequently endured suffering at the hands of his captors as a continuation and overflow of his act of identification with his people who saw no clear end to their misery at the hand of the system."[14]

For Filipino women Jesus is neither a masochist who enjoys suffering, nor a father's boy who blindly does what he is told to do. On the contrary, Jesus is a compassionate man of integrity who identified himself with the oppressed. He "stood for all he taught and did" and took responsibility for the consequences of his choice even at the price of his life. This image of Jesus' suffering gives Asian women the wisdom to differentiate between the suffering imposed by an oppressor and the suffering that is the consequence of one's stand for justice and human dignity.

Korean theologian Choi Man Ja makes this liberative aspect of Jesus' suffering clear in her presentation on feminist Christology. She asks this question: "How do women who are in the situation of suffering under and obeying oppressive power, take on significance as suffering and obeying servants?"[15] Her answer is:

Suffering is not an end in itself, ... it has definite social references of divine redemptive activity. Suffering exposes patriarchal evil. Jesus endures the yoke of the cross against the evil powers of this patriarchal world. This obedience is different from simple submission to the worldly authority.[16]

Another Korean woman theologian, Park Soon Kyung, developed further the meaning of Jesus' servanthood. According to her, Jesus' servanthood changed the meaning of being a slave among the oppressed people. The yoke of slaves is proof of the world's injustice and witness to the desire for God's righteousness.[17] Therefore, servanthood is not mere submission or obedience. It is instead a powerful witness to evil and a challenge to the powers and the principalities of the world, especially male domination over women. This suffering servant who is undergoing passive suffering with powerless Asian women and who is also accompanying them in their struggle for liberation by doing liberation is the prophetic Messiah who creates a new humanity for oppressed Asian women. Through Jesus Christ, Asian women see new meaning in their suffering and service. They see life-giving aspects in their suffering and service that create a new humanity for the people they serve.

Jesus as Lord

If the liberative dimension of the suffering servant image frees Asian women from imposed suffering and empowers them to accept suffering as a consequence of their own choice for liberation, the liberative dimension of the Lord image of Jesus frees Asian women from the false authority of the world over them and empowers them to claim true authority which springs from life-giving experiences.

Yet like the image of the suffering servant, the image of Lord also has been used against Asian women, perpetuating their submissive and oppressed status in Asian society and the church. Traditionally Asian women have not been the owners of themselves under mainline patriarchal culture. In the East Asian context where Confucianism was the dominant social and religious ideology, women have had to obey the men in their lives: fathers before marriage, husbands in marriage, and sons in widowhood. The Asian woman's man was her lord. In addition to Confucianism, feudalism and the emperor system did not give much space for the self-determination of women. Even though women could not actively participate in any public or political affairs, they did, of course, suffer from the results of the hierarchical social system (in such concrete ways as lack of food due to oppressive taxes).

Western colonialism used Jesus' image as Lord to justify political and economic domination over many Asian countries. Western missionaries tried to brainwash Asian people by identifying the Western colonizer's Lord Jesus with the Lord for Asians, claiming that the colonizer's Lord Jesus was ruler of the whole universe. Therefore to become a Christian meant obeying the Lord Jesus and the colonial power which brought him to Asia.

This ruler image of Lord Jesus became especially strong in countries like the Philippines which were colonized by Spain. The Spanish conquistadores put Lord Jesus over all the indigenous spirits in the Philippines and put their king over the tribal leadership of the Filipino people. In their recent research many Filipino women theologians have begun to name this lordship ideology of colonial Christianity and its impact on Filipino women's lives.[18] They demonstrate that the lordship ideology of colonial Christianity domesticated the vibrant pre-colonial Filipino women's self-understanding and power in the community.[19] Filipino women shared equally or with even more power than men in domestic and public life before Spanish colonialism. Filipino women were active members in local politics and economics. According to Mary John Mananzan's research, even some male scholars believe that Filipino society was based on a matriarchal culture before colonization.[20] This active image of the power of Filipino women was diminished as Christianity was spread along with the feudal ideology of the colonial power. The ideal image of the Filipino woman became one of passivity, submissiveness, obedience, and chastity.

Under this historical reality many Asian women who were seeking women's liberation and self-determination have become suspicious of the Lord image of Jesus. Yet they also see the liberative power of the image of Jesus as Lord of the poor and oppressed women in Asia. One of the most articulate voices who illustrate this point is Park Soon Kyung from Korea. She is fully aware of ruler ideology (*Herren Ideologie*) of the image of Jesus as Lord, but she asserts that the lordship of Jesus is "the exact opposite" of patriarchal lordship.[21] For her, the lordship of Jesus means the lordship of justice, which "judges the evil power of rulers in this world."[22] While patriarchal lordship of this world means the ruling power that oppresses people, lordship of Jesus means the power that liberates people. The concept of power and authority in Jesus' lordship is completely different from that in patriarchal lordship. Jesus' lordship is the lordship of the "creator and savior of human and nature."[23] The title *Kyrios* (Lord), which was the word for ruler in Hellenistic culture, transformed its meaning radically when it was used to name the power of Jesus. According to Park Soon Kyung, the lordship of Jesus which comes from God limits the lordship of the rulers in this world by showing the real meaning of lordship through Jesus' deeds and his eschatological vision. All lordship in this world "should return to its origin," which is God.[24] Therefore, all lordship in this world becomes "relativized" under the eschatological vision of Jesus. The lordship in this world should be "the means which serves the salvation of humankind" and "the righteousness and providence of God."[25] Park says:

> The Lordship of Christ means that his Lordship is exact opposite of patriarchal Lordship and he eschatologically places the rule of the evil powers in this world under God's judgement. Jesus put a period to the power of patriarchal history by obeying to the righteousness of God as a male even to his death. His Lordship is the Lordship of the righteousness of God which is established by his suffering and death. This Lordship destroys the principality and power of the world and returns all the power and authority to God.[26]

Jesus' lordship, then, says no to patriarchal domination, freeing Asian women from false authority and empowering them to obey only God and not men.

Jesus as Immanuel (God-with-us)

Jesus, who became the Lord of the universe through his suffering and service for humanity, also shows Asian women God's presence among them. Many Asian women cherish the mystery of the incarnation through Jesus' person and work. "Both the human and divine nature of Jesus are important" for Asian women's identity and mission.[27] Their understanding of Jesus' humanity and divinity, however, is very different from that of Nicene-Chalcedonian theological definitions stressing the Son's relationship to the Father and the two natures of his person. Asian women's concern for the humanity and divinity of Jesus derives from their resistance to colonial, male domination in their churches and cultures. Two distinguished voices which articulate the meaning of incarnation (Logos becoming flesh in Jesus) come from India and Korea. Indian theologian Monica Melanchton and Korean theologian Lee Oo Chung, express the meaning of incarnation and Immanuel from their specific socio-political and religio-cultural contexts.

Monica Melanchton locates Jesus' divinity in his sinlessness, virgin birth, resurrection, and "the tremendous authority Jesus claimed and exercised."[28] She explains Jesus' divine power further:

> The thing that impressed the masses was that the teaching of Jesus was differentiated from that of the Scribes by its innate sense of authority. It was with this power vested in him that he performed exorcism, forgave sins, healed the sick and preached with authority. That any mere human could claim such authority and back it up with his actions is beyond the remotest possibility. Hence every New Testament book attributes deity/divinity to Jesus either by direct statement or by inference.[29]

But this Jesus also shares human finitude with us by "lying in the cradle, growing, learning, feeling the pangs of hunger, thirst, anxiety, doubt, grief, and finally death and burial."[30] For Melanchton, Jesus is a "representative"[31] of the reality of "God-with-us"(Immanuel). She claims, however, that the institutional church distorted Jesus' image by emphasizing his maleness rather than his humanity. Jesus' maleness became "a constitutive factor in deciding the place and role of women."[32] Jesus' maleness excluded women from full participation in the church. She emphasizes that through his incarnation Jesus becomes the representative of a new humanity, not only of men, who are just one-half of the human race, but of women too. Melanchton warns that emphasizing the maleness of Jesus is a pagan act.

> If we ascribe maleness to Jesus Christ, we are also committing the mistake of ascribing the pagan/Hindu notions of sexuality to our God who transcends this. The Church in India needs to recognize the personhood of Jesus Christ and the fact that Christ is the representative human being for all people including Indian women.[33]

For her, Jesus' humanity embraces all people. The Christian God transcends sexuality and therefore frees Indian women from the stereotypical role assignments in Indian culture. Jesus as the Immanuel (God-with-us) transforms Hindu culture.

In contrast to Melanchton, Lee Oo Chung shows how Korean culture transforms the meaning of Immanuel, incarnation, and the divinity and humanity of Jesus. Lee Oo Chung advocates a Christology from below in a Korean context. According to her the traditional concept of Korean gods in general is that "special persons having done special things in a lifetime, become gods after death."[34] There is a popular format for these special persons becoming gods:

1) The issue of noble family
2) Extraordinary birth
3) Extraordinary childhood

4) Becoming an orphan at an early age or facing other kinds of suffering

5) Being rescued from the situation or surviving by encountering foster parents

6) Facing a crisis again

7) Winning a victory by fighting and obtaining glory.[35]

The above format is often seen in the stories of heroes who became gods. However, interestingly enough, when the story is about heroines, it has similar steps up to the sixth stage but "in the end she wins victory to become a god by suffering, loving, being patient, and sacrificing instead of fighting."[36] There are many gods in Korea who ascended to the position of god from being human through his or her love, suffering, and sacrifice. Among them, the majority are female.[37]

In this cultural framework Christology from above (God become human) is difficult to understand for the ordinary masses of people (minjung), especially laborers. Conceptual and abstract images of God in Christian theology, such as "totally other," "unmovable mover," and "immutable, impassable, unchangeable God," do not make much sense to Korean people. Lee Oo Chung observes Korean people's understanding of Jesus:

> The doctrine of God's becoming a man is a hard proposition for them [Korean Minjung] to accept. However "A man becomes a god" is easy for them to understand. Jesus Christ as Messiah can be better understood in the image of historical Jesus who has loved his neighbors more than himself and for this great love he went through surmounting suffering and sacrifice to become the Messiah, the Savior of humankind. Whereas the theory which says that because Jesus was God he was Messiah does not appeal too much.[38]

Lee proposes a radical task of liberation for Korean Christian women: In order to fully "experience the mystery of doctrine of incarnation by choice," Korean women must get out of the imposed service role in the church and society. This is possible when Korean women "elevate our self-consciousness as high as in the realm of the divine."[39] This elevation of women's self-consciousness will be generated from women's "experience of real love of God, for our totality of being the body, mind, and soul, as an individual and as a social being."[40]

Korean women experience the mystery of incarnation and "God-with-us" by becoming like Jesus. Many Korean Christians in the movement claim that we should become "little Jesuses" in order to become true Christians. For many Korean women, Jesus is not the objectified divine being whom people must worship. Rather, Jesus is the one we relive through our lives. The meaning of Immanuel, then, has been changed through Korean mythological symbols and language from God-*with*-us to God-*among*-us, and finally to God-*is*-us in our struggle to reclaim our full humanity.

New Emerging Images

New images of Jesus have emerged from Asian women's movements for self-determination and liberation. The freer Asian women become from the patriarchal authorities of their family, church, and society, the more creative they become in naming their experience of Jesus Christ. Sometimes the images of Jesus are transformed to the degree that they show the radical discontinuity between the ones found in the Jewish and Christian culture and those from the Asian women's movement. Some Asian women have become confident enough in themselves to name the presence of Jesus Christ in their own culture, indigenous religions, and secular political movements, a Christological identity that is not directly connected in the traditional sense with Christianity. They use religio-political symbols and motifs from their movement in order to describe what Jesus means for them in today's Asia. This is a *Christological transformation* created out of Asian women's experiences as they struggle for full humanity. The old Christological paradigms are transformed, new meanings are achieved, and diverse images of Jesus Christ emerge. Asian women as meaning-makers jump into an unknown open future shaping a new Christianity out of their own experience that never before existed in history. The following are examples of new, emerging images of Jesus Christ derived from Asian women who believe in their historical lived experience more than imposed authority.

Jesus as Liberator, Revolutionary, and Political Martyr
Jesus Christ is portrayed as liberator in many writings of women from various Asian countries such as India, Indonesia, Korea, the Philippines, and Sri Lanka. The reason why Jesus as liberator is the most prominent new image among Asian women is a consequence of their historical situation. The liberation from colonialism, neo-colonialism, poverty, and military dictatorship, as well as from overarching patriarchy, has been the major aspiration of twentieth-century Asian women.

In the composite paper of the EATWOT Asian Women's Consultation, entitled "Women and the Christ Event," Jesus is defined as "the prototype of the real liberator."[41] They also claim that Jesus as liberator is evident "in the image of liberators in other non-christian religions and movements."[42] A participant at the consultation, Pauline Hensman, a woman theologian from Sri Lanka, described Jesus Christ as the one who "came with good news to the poor, oppressed and downtrodden" and through whom "humankind was released from servitude and alienation by those who dominated and oppressed them."[43] This image of Jesus Christ as liberator is made concrete as revolutionary or political martyr in the Filipino women's reflection on the Christ event presented at the same consultation. According to Lydia Lascano from the Philippines, Filipino women who participate in the people's struggle for liberation "live out with their lives the Christ event—Jesus' life, passion, death and resurrection—leaving the mark of their womenhood in the Philippine liberation project, the project of God."[44]

Filipino women have suffered (under more than three hundred years of Spanish and American colonialism and military dictatorships) and have resisted in order to survive and reclaim their human dignity as a people. Filipino women find Christ's suffering, death and resurrection *in* the suffering, death, and resurrection of Filipino women themselves. They see revolutionary acts of Christ among "the militant protesting Filipino women who have taken up the struggle for themselves and for the rest of the Filipino nation."[45] In their organized action for liberation, Filipino women have been arrested, raped, tortured, imprisoned, and displaced from their homes. Many have even been killed in their struggle toward self-determination for their people. Their names are today remembered by women in protest movements. Some names include:

> Lorena Barros, a freedom fighter; Filomena Asuncion, a deaconess who offered her life for the conscientization of peasants; Leticia Celestino, a factory worker shot in the picketlines while demanding for a just wage; Angelina Sayat, a freedom fighter who died while in the custody of the military; Puri Pedro, a Catechist who served the farmers, was tortured and killed while being treated in a hospital.[46]

In the death of those political martyrs for freedom is the death of Jesus. Unlike the women of Jerusalem in Jesus' time, women are not just comforting or shedding tears for Jesus on his way to the cross. Filipino women shed blood for their people. Sister Lascano explains the political martyrdom among Filipino women:

> Today, the passion of Christ in the Filipino people is fashioning women disciples who would accompany the suffering Christ alive among the people, not merely to comfort and support but even to die with them. In the passion for social transformation, death takes on a new level of meaningfulness. . . . Today many Filipino women do not merely accompany Christ to Calvary as spectators. They carry the cross with him and undergo his passion in an act of identification with his suffering.[47]

The resurrection of Jesus comes alive in the resurrection of these martyrs. The Filipino women's resistance movement makes the spirit and vision of these martyrs come alive by persistent "organized action" and "active waiting and watching" for the future victory of the struggle.[48] When poor Filipino women are awakened to see the root cause of their suffering in structural evils, they begin to claim for themselves land and rights as human beings. They utter in discovery, "We will also have our Exodus!"[49] And they take political action. This discovery has stirred hope in their hearts, believing that "the liberating God of the Exodus has become alive in the resurrected Christ, now alive among them as *the Bagong Kristo* (the New Christ)."[50]

Jesus as Mother, Woman, and Shaman

Many Asian women portray Jesus with the image of mother. They see Jesus as a compassionate one who feels the suffering of humanity deeply, suffers and weeps with them. Since Jesus' compassion is so deep, the mother image is the most appropriate one for Asian women to express their experience of Jesus' compassion. Hong Kong theologian Kwok Pui-lan explains this point in her essay, "God Weeps with Our Pain":

> Jesus cried out for Jerusalem. His sorrow was so deep Matthew had to use a "feminine metaphor" to describe what he actually felt: How often would I have gathered your children together as a hen gathers her brood under her wings (Matt. 23:37).[51]

Like a mother who laments over her dead son who died in the wars in Indochina, like many weeping Korean mothers whose sons and daughters were taken by the secret police, Jesus cried out for the pain of suffering humanity. Korean theologian Lee Oo Chung questions why Jesus suffered so keenly before his death.[52] Even Jesus says to the disciples: "The sorrow in my heart is so great that it almost crushes me. Stay here and keep watch." Jesus was not like one of those saints and heroes who died calmly and serenely. According to Lee, Jesus was different from those saints and heroes because they "bore only their own suffering while Jesus took on himself the pain and suffering of all his neighbors, even of all humankind."[53]

Like some of Jesus' disciples, people who were only interested in the expansion of their personal glory, honor, and power ("When you sit on your throne in your glorious kingdom, we want you to let us sit with you, one at your right and one at your left"—Mark 10:37) could not feel the pain of the suffering poor nor see the violence and evil of the oppressors.[54] Jesus was different from them in that he felt the pain of all humanity like a compassionate mother. Lee discovers the image of Jesus as a compassionate mother who really feels the hurt and pain of her child in Korean folklore:

> In the National Museum in Kyungju, Korea, capital of the ancient Silla Kingdom, is a beautiful bell. The Silla Kingdom at the time enjoyed peace, but the King, a devout Buddhist, wanted to protect his people from foreign invasion. His advisors suggested that he build a huge temple bell to show the people's devotion to the Buddha.
>
> A specialist in the art of bellmaking was commissioned. But despite his skill and care, he failed time and again to produce a bell with a

beautiful sound. Finally, he went back to the council of religious leaders. After a long discussion, they concluded that the best way to give a beautiful tone to the bell was to sacrifice a pure young maiden.

Soldiers were sent to find and fetch such a young girl. Coming upon a poor mother in a farm village with her small daughter, they took the child away, while she cried out piteously: "Emille, Emille!" — "Mother! O Mother!" When the molten lead and iron were prepared, the little girl was thrown in. At last the bellmaker suceeded. The bell, called the Emille Bell, made a sound more beautiful than any other.

When it rang, most people praised the art that had produced such a beautiful sound. But whenever the mother whose child had been sacrificed heard it, her heart broke anew.[55]

For Lee, Jesus is like the little girl's mother. Jesus' heart breaks anew when he hears the cry of humanity. People who do not know the meaning of sacrifice enjoy the achievement based on other people's sacrifice. But people "who understand the sacrifice can feel the pain."[56] This image of Jesus shows Asian women that the redemption of humankind "has not come through those who are comfortable and unconcerned, but only through the One who shared the suffering of all humankind."[57]

This compassionate, sensitive mother image of Jesus was shared by the Indonesian theologian Marianne Katoppo. She illustrates her point by quoting a prayer of Anselm and a poem from the Indian poet Narayan Vaman Tilak:

And thou, Jesus, sweet Lord, art Thou not also a mother?
Truly, Thou art a mother, the mother of all mothers
Who tasted death, in Thy desire to give life to Thy children
— Anselm[58]

Tenderest Mother-Guru mine,
Saviour, where is love like thine?
— Narayan Vaman Tilak[59]

This mother image of Jesus demolishes "the paternalistic, authoritarian and hierarchical patterns" in our life and builds the "maternal, compassionate, sensitive, bearing and upbearing" relationship among people.[60]

Some Asian women see Jesus Christ as a female figure in their specific historical situation. Two articulate voices on this position are found in Korea. Park Soon Kyung concluded her Christology at the gathering of the Korean Association of Women Theologians by saying that even though Jesus has a male physical form, he is "a symbol of females and the oppressed" due to his identification with the one who hurts the most. Therefore, on a symbolic level, we may call Jesus the *"woman Messiah"* who is the liberator of the oppressed.[61] She claims justification for naming

Jesus' humanity as female in the current historical situation because Christology needs to be liberated from the patriarchal church structure.

Choi Man Ja goes one step further by identifying Korean women's historical struggle for liberation with "the praxis of messiahship."[62] She says, "Even though women are excluded from the ordained ministry, in fact women are the true praxis of messiah-Jesus, in Korea."[63] For her, Jesus' messiahship comes from his suffering servantship. Therefore, she can recognize the praxis of new humanity most clearly through a female messiah who is in the suffering and struggle of Asian women. This female Christ is "the new humanity, siding with the oppressed, and liberating women from their suffering."[64]

Another female image of Jesus comes from the image of the shaman. Virginia Fabella shares her learning from Korean women in her article "Asian Women and Christology."[65] Under oppressive political and economic oppression, and under the added burden of the Confucian system of ethics which inculcates male domination, Korean women's life experience is *han* itself. The resentment, indignation, sense of defeat, resignation, and nothingness in *han* make many Korean women brokenhearted and physically sick. In this situation, what would be the significance of Jesus Christ for them? Fabella cites an answer from a Korean woman: "If Jesus Christ is to make sense to us, then Jesus Christ must be a priest of Han" for minjung women.[66] For the minjung women, salvation and redemption means being exorcised from their accumulated *han*, untangling of their many-layered *han*. Since Korean indigenous religion is shamanism, Korean women easily accept the Jesus of the synoptic gospels, who exorcised and healed the sick and possessed like a Korean shaman. As the Korean shaman has been a healer, comforter, and counselor for Korean women, Jesus Christ healed and comforted women in his ministry.

In Korea the majority of shamans are women. Shamanism is the only religion among the various Korean religious traditions where women have been the center all through its development. Women shamans have been "big sisters" to many deprived minjung women, untangling their *han* and helping them cope with life's tribulations.[67] When Korean women, therefore, see Jesus Christ as the priest of *han*, they connect with the female image of Jesus more than the male image of Jesus. They take Jesus as a big sister just as they take the shaman as a big sister in their community.

The female image of Jesus Christ is expressed most vividly by a theologian in India, Gabriele Dietrich,[68] who makes a connection between women's menstruation and Jesus' shedding of blood on the cross. She sees the meaning of the Eucharist in women's monthly bloodshed. She expresses her point powerfully through her poem:

> I am a woman
> and my blood
> cries out:

Who are you
to deny life
to the life-givers?
Each one of you
has come from the womb
but none of you
can bear woman
when she is strong
and joyful and competent.
You want our tears
to clamour for protection.
Who are you
to protect us
from yourselves?

I am a woman
and my monthly bloodshed
makes me aware
that blood
is meant for life.
It is you
who have invented
those lethal machines
spreading death:
Three kilotonnes of explosives
for every human being
on earth.

I am a woman
and the blood
of my abortions
is crying out.
I had to kill
my child
because of you
who deny work to me
so that i cannot feed it.
I had to kill my child
because i am unmarried
and you would harass me
to death
if i defy
your norms.

I am a woman
and the blood

of being raped
is crying out.
This is how you keep
your power intact,
how you make me tremble
when i go out at night.
This is how you keep
me in place
in my house where
you rape me again.
I am not taking this
any longer.

I am a woman
and the blood
of my operation
is crying out.
Even if i am a nun
you still use my body
to make money
by giving me a hysterectomy
when i don't need it.
My body is in the clutches
of husbands, policemen,
doctors, pimps.
There is no end
to my alienation.

I am a woman
and the blood
of my struggles
is crying out.
Yes, my comrades,
you want us
in the forefront
because you have learnt
you cannot do without us.
You need us
in the class struggle
as you need us
in bed and to cook
your grub
to bear
your children to dress
your wounds.

You will celebrate
women's day
like mother's day
garlands
for our great supporters.
Where would we be
without our women?

I am a woman
and the blood
of my sacrifices
cries out to the sky
which you call heaven.
I am sick of you priests
who have never bled
and yet say:
This is my body
given up for you
and my blood
shed for you
drink it.
Whose blood
has been shed
for life
since eternity?
I am sick of you priests
who rule the *garbagriha,*
who adore the womb
as a source for life
and keep me shut out
because my blood
is polluting.

I am a woman
and i keep bleeding
from my womb
but also from my heart
because it is difficult
to learn to hate
and it might not help
if i hate you.

I still love
my little son
who bullies his sister.

He has learnt it outside,
how do i stop him?
I still love
my children's father
because he was there
when i gave birth.
I still long
for my lover's touch
to break the spell
of perversion
which has grown
like a wall
between women and men.
I still love
my comrades in arms
because they care
for others who suffer
and there is hope
that they give their bodies
in the struggle for life
and not just for power.
But i have learned
to love my sisters.
We have learned
to love one another.
We have learned
even to respect
ourselves.

I am a woman
and my blood
cries out.
We are millions
and strong together.
You better hear us
or you may be doomed.

Dietrich questions the hypocrisy of the patriarchal church and society which "deny life to the life-givers." They "adore the womb as a source" but shut out women from full participation in life. The womb is praised but not those who have wombs. Most of the so-called higher world religions condemn women's menstruation as dirty or polluting. Women cannot preside in the ritual of many religions because their monthly flow will "corrupt" holy altars. Dietrich asks Christian priests who worship the holy blood-shedding of Jesus: "Whose blood has been shed for life since eternity?"

Then she claims priests, not women, "have never bled and yet say: this is my body given up for you and my blood shed for you, drink it." Jesus shed blood on the cross due to his solidarity with the poor, oppressed, and alienated. He bled so as to give others everlasting life. Like Jesus, women's blood has been shed from eternity. Women's menstruation is a holy Eucharist through which the renewal of life becomes possible. Jesus joins women in his life-giving bleeding.[69]

Jesus as Worker and Grain

Female images of Jesus Christ enable Asian women to image Jesus on the earth. The revelation of God they have heard from the church is usually the revelation from above. Theology based on the revelation from above can easily be distorted into a theology of domination because this theology is based on the abstract thinking of the head and not on the concrete experience of the body. It is based on distant (and largely male) intellectualism and not on the everyday, experiential reality of Asian women. Some Asian women find Jesus in the most ordinary, everyday experience. They see the revelation of God from below, the bottom, the earth. They refuse any kind of heroism. They are not looking for great men and women to worship. Rather, they want to find God, the saving presence within their daily lives.

A witness of faith from a Korean factory worker shows the meaning of Jesus Christ among the ordinary poor people:

I don't know how to live a Christ-like life. But I am discovering and awakening to the meaning of it little by little in my daily life. This is a cautious and mysterious process. [In order to explain this point,] I would like to talk about my mother. She is a woman full of "Han." She describes herself like that. She was married when she was seventeen. She gave birth to three children. Then her husband died even before she became thirty. Now my mother gets up 4:30 a.m. every morning and goes to marketplace for banding. There are too many people in the marketplace. It is hard to walk there. I think that marketplace is truly our context of life.

From early morning my mother carries heavy bundles and walks around the marketplace distributing the vinyl bags used for wrapping to banders and stores. She gathers the money from them later. That work is too strenuous for a woman of my mother's age and physical strength. Therefore, whenever she happens to have a holiday (like a full moon festival), she becomes sick and has to stay in bed. Her shoulder becomes unbalanced and her back is bent. Her cheek becomes red with ice since she has to work outside in the cold winter. Her life seems like a tired, hard, and insignificant one.

Whenever I see my mother, her face reminds me of the tired faces of my friends in the factory who are working eighteen to twenty-four hours a day without even any facial expression. Workers do not stop their work even when they are overwhelmed by despair and disgust. And workers really know how to love other people. Since they experience despair, are humiliated by the rich and endure miserable situations, they know how to love the people in despair under every circumstance—even though we are in despair all the time. The world is constructed out of these hearts.

When I see workers, I feel the breath and heart-beat of history and the meaning of humanity and Christ in them. I think we will not be saved without workers because workers truly have the loving power and unbeatable endurance. I wonder how Jesus the Christ will look when he comes back again. When I was young, I dreamt about Jesus wearing silverly white clothing, accompanying many angels with bright light and great sounds of music. But now I wonder. If Jesus comes again, he may come to us wearing ragged clothing and give my tired mother, who even dozes off while she is standing, a bottle of *Bakas*[70] or he may come to me, working mindlessly in the noisy factory, and quietly help my work while wearing an oily worker's uniform. I think *our Christ is the ground of life, and my faith is in the midst of this working life and workers.*[71]

This factory worker sees her Christ in workers and their hard struggle for survival. She does not believe any longer in the image of a flamboyant Jesus who looks like one of the rich and famous people in her childhood. She finds Jesus in her fellow workers who endure despair, humiliation, and back-breaking hard work, yet share their love and resources with other workers. Jesus Christ does not descend from glorious-looking heaven; Christ emerges from the broken-body experience of workers when they affirm life and dare to love other human beings in spite of their brokenness. Workers become Christ to each other when they touch each other's wounds and heal each other through sharing food, work, and hope.

Another image of Jesus Christ which emerges from the earth is found in a poem from an Indian woman. She meets her Jesus Christ when she receives two hundred grams of gruel in a famine-stricken area. For her, Christ, God's beloved Son, is food for hungry people.

> Every noon at twelve
> In the blazing heat
> God comes to me
> in the form of
> Two hundred grams of gruel.
>
> I know Him in every grain
> I taste Him in every lick.
> I commune with Him as I gulp

For He keeps me alive, with
Two hundred grams of gruel.

I wait till next noon
and now know He'd come:
I can hope to live one day more
For you made God to come to me as
Two hundreds grams of gruel.

I know now that God loves me—
Not until you made it possible.
Now I know what you're speaking about
For God so loves this world
That He gives His beloved Son
Every noon through You.[72]

Without food, there is no life. When starving people eat the food, they experience God "in every grain." They "know" and "taste" God when they chew each grain. Food makes them alive. The greatest love of God for the starving people is food. When the grain from the earth sustains their life, they discover the meaning of the phrase, "For God so loves this world that He gives His beloved Son." When God gives them food through other concerned human beings, God gives them God's "beloved Son," Jesus Christ.

In conclusion, we have observed that there are *traditional* images of Jesus, which are being interpreted in fresh, creative ways by Asian women, largely based on their experiences of survival in the midst of oppression and on their efforts to liberate themselves. We also have observed *new* images of Jesus that offer a direct challenge to traditional Christologies. These new images of Jesus are also based on Asian women's experiences of survival and liberation. Because Jesus was a male, however, some Asian women think there is a limit to how much he can be transformed to meet the needs of Asian women. This is the main reason why Asian women theologians have emphasized the importance of Mary in their recent writings. We turn next to Mary in our examination of emerging Asian women's theology.

5

WHO IS MARY
FOR TODAY'S ASIAN WOMEN?

What have you done to me? What have you made of me?
I cannot find myself in the woman you want me to be . . .
Haloed, alone . . . marble and stone: Safe, Gentle, Holy
   Mary.

My sisters, look at me! Don't turn in pain from me.
Your lives and mine are one in rage and agony . . .
Silenced, denied, or sanctified . . . Safe, Gentle, Holy Mary.

Revolution is my song! MAGNIFICAT proclaims it!
The promise that it makes to us, we dare now to reclaim
   it!
In our weakness we are strong: wise through pain and grief
   and wrong . . .
Giving, loving, angry women.

All generations will acclaim me only if you can acclaim
   me . . .
Live with joy the truth you find—woman—this is what you
   name me:
Suffering, proud, prophetic, unbowed . . .
Whole, laughing, daughter . . . Mary:
Real, warm, living woman . . . Mary:
THEN I will be WHOLLY Mary![1]

If Jesus, a Jewish man, became a symbol of new humanity for Asian
women, transcending historical, geographical, and gender boundaries, so
Mary, a Jewish woman, also became another symbol of new humanity for
Asian women through her words and deeds. Jesus and Mary, therefore, are

74

two models of the fully liberated human being from whom Asian Christian women find their source of empowerment and inspiration. Yet many Asian women feel closer to Mary as a model for full humanity than to Jesus for the obvious reason that Mary is a woman. In most Asian churches where the maleness of Jesus has been used against women in order to legitimize the sexist ideology of women's inferiority, women have found comfort and self-worth through the presence of Mary, an invaluable woman for human salvation. But Mary's presence has not always been empowering to Asian women. Until recently, before Asian women began a united effort to reclaim their power and dignity as full human beings, Mary was used against Asian women. In some cases various negative Mariologies were invented by the patriarchal church to justify women's subordination to men. In other cases Mary was eliminated by the church so women would have no model of a truly liberated woman.

Asian women think that the Protestant tradition's repudiation of Mariology and its imposition of an all-male theology shows the church's "avoidance of responsibility to address women's place in realistic terms."[2] Under this attitude of the church Asian women have been "forced to be altered to Jesus/Christology through male eyes"[3] as the sole model for full humanity. Therefore, the rightful woman's place has been denied in the Protestant church.

If the Protestant church has succeeded in oppressing women by eliminating Mary, the Catholic church has exercised control over women by domesticating Mary. On the one hand, Mary is exalted as "the Beloved Virgin" and "Mother of God" when virgin motherhood is a "biological impossibility."[4] By making Mary the "Virgin Mother," the patriarchal church made Mary into an exceptional woman with whom no ordinary women could identify. "Virgin Mother" shows the "fear and degradation of birthing and female sexuality"[5] of the male-dominated church.

On the other hand, Mary is tamed as a passive, obedient, yes-woman or humble maid who does everything men want. She is "sugar-sweet, fragile, with eyes either modestly downcast or upturned to heaven — not quite here-and-now!"[6] Then she is saying: "I am the Lord's servant, may it happen to me as you have said." This shows the ultimate Catholic male fantasy of "femininity" or of "what the ideal women should be." This Mary is a symbol of a woman who is domesticated by men. She is a derived human being according to men's need and not a "human being in her own right."[7] That is why the ritualistic adoration of Mary in the Catholic church is expressed as "daughter of the Father, mother of Jesus, spouse of the Holy Spirit."[8] She has value only when she is attached to men as daughter, mother, or spouse. This image of Mary domesticated Asian women to fit the needs of men under colonialism and capitalism. Women became "programmed to forgive [men] or blame ourselves for violence against us, never to express anger or fight back."[9]

Male-defined Mary has been a *familiar alien* for Asian women from the

time she was introduced to them. Mary's life story as a woman, her suffering, and her love for her own son, sound "familiar" to Asian women. But
Mary is also an "alien" to Asian women because she either is too clean,
too high, and too holy or she is too sweet, too passive, and too forgiving
for Asian women to make any meaningful connection with her *as women*.
This Mary is outside Asian women's bodily experience. She is "haloed and
alone in marble and stone."[10] This Mary only deepens the scar of Asian
women's schizophrenia caused by patriarchal domination. Paradoxically,
Asian women feel shame because they cannot be as clean (virginal chastity)
as Mary, and they feel guilty because they cannot be as good as Mary. And
yet Asian women feel compelled to imitate Mary because she represents
"what is acceptably female."[11] When Mary is placed as a norm for "ideal
womanhood" outside of Asian women's everyday, concrete, bodily experience, she becomes a source of disempowerment for Asian women. One
young Indian Christian woman shares her frustration with the traditional
image of Mary:

> For a long time, Mary and I were strangers. I respected her as the
> mother of Jesus, but I just could not identify with the passive, col-
> ourless virgin she was made out to be. As a human being constantly
> struggling through difficult choices I could find no comfort in this
> docile Mary who said "Yes" so easily to God. As a young woman
> faced with the challenge of taking up my rightful role in society, I just
> could not understand this Mary tucked away inside her four walls.
> She was the "virgin most pure" with whom I could never share the
> excitement of my flowering sexuality. What could this sinless woman
> understand of my weakness and failures?[12]

While resonating with this young woman's frustration, Asian women also
claim their right and responsibility to rediscover Mary as liberator. In the
"Summary Statement on Mariology" from the Consultation of Asian Wom-
en's Theology held in Singapore in 1987 Asian women defined the twofold
task of feminist Mariology:

> 1) We must name, and liberate ourselves from, the destructive efforts
> of two thousand years of male interpretation of Mary.
> 2) We must return to the Scriptures as women within our own
> cultural contexts, to re-discover the Mary who is liberated and liber-
> ator.[13]

Asian women's feminist perspectives on Mary are redeeming the
"silenced, denied, sanctified, safe, gentle, holy Mary" from "her marble and
stone" prison through Asian women's anger and revolutionary action.[14] Let
us look at the liberated and liberator image of Mary which is being created
out of Asian women's womb of suffering and wisdom.

Mary as a Model for Full Womanhood and of the Fully Liberated Human Being

Mary as Virgin: Self-Defining Woman

Asian women are beginning to view the virginity of Mary, not as a *biological* reality, but as a *relational* reality. Indonesian theologian Marianne Katoppo articulates this point. For her, Mary's virginity means she is a "liberated human being, who—not being subject to any other human being—is free to serve God."[15] Virginity lies in her true connectedness to her own self and to God. It is "an inner attitude, not a psychological or external fact."[16] When a woman defines herself according to her own understanding of who she really is and what she is meant for in this universe (and not according to the rules and norms of patriarchy), she is a virgin. Therefore, her virginity persists "in spite of sexual experience, child bearing and increasing age."[17] Actually her virginity, her ability to be a self-defining woman, grows because of her full range of life experience.

Virgin is "the symbol for the autonomy of women."[18] Virgin primarily means not "a woman who abstains from sexual intercourse" but a woman who does not lead a derived life, as "daughter/wife/mother" of men.[19] She is a "woman who matures to wholeness within herself as a complete person, and who is open for others."[20]

Han Kuk Yum, a Korean woman theologian, pushes the meaning of virginity one step further. Quoting another Korean woman theologian, Park Soon Kyung, she argues that Mary's virgin birth of Jesus means that "the human-male is excluded" from this important event of the birth of new humanity.

> The fact that in Jesus' birth, human-male is excluded connotes that a new human image, a new saving world could no longer be sustained through a patriarchal order. The human-saving Messiah who saves humanity has nothing to do with the patriarchal view of value or patriarchal order, but is totally the birth of new human image.[21]

The virgin birth, then, means the overture of the end of the patriarchal order. It is the symbol of God's judgment against men's sinning against women. Through the event of the virgin birth, God shows men that they cannot control and oppress women. This event also shows women that salvation is sufficient without men. The church's emphasis, therefore, of the virgin birth as a miraculous, clean birth that is not "corrupted" by human sexuality only shows its sickness as "a marked sexual neurosis."[22] Korean theologian Han thinks that if the miraculous virgin birth is important for the patriarchal church, it would be more convincing for them to insist that Jesus was born from an egg rather than a woman's body.[23] For many Asian women Mary's virginity is an active symbol of resistance against patriarchal order. Mary as a virgin is a complete human being within herself. She defines her life. By defining herself by her experience and her faith in God (and not by patriarchal norms), she becomes a model of full womanhood and liberated humanity for many Asian women.

Mary as Mother: Giver of Life to God and New Humanity

Since Mary is a virgin who is not domesticated by the patriarchal order, she can give birth to God and new humanity. The new order of God, the new redeemed humanity, cannot be brought to the world through the old order of patriarchy, which is based on the principle of domination. By defying the patriarchal order in her decision to have a child out of wedlock, and by her believing in God and herself, Mary enables God to be born through her own body. Mary matures to wholeness by believing in God and herself and through her openness to an unknown future. "Through this maturing process, she is *fertile*, she *gives life* for God."[24]

Mary's giving birth to both the Messiah and to a new humanity starts with her saying yes to God's plan for salvation for a broken humanity. This affirmation of God's plan through her motherhood of Jesus and the new humanity is not mere obedience and submission to a male God but a conscious choice on her part. Mary's choice is based on her historical consciousness "as a young Jewish girl thoroughly steeped in the traditions of Israel and the historical struggle of her people."[25] With fear and trembling she takes the risk of participating in God's plan out of her vision of redeemed humanity. Mary takes this risk not as a heroic superwoman, but as an ordinary woman who is receptive to God's calling, which draws her from her own private safety. She is fully aware of the consequences of her choice: social ostracism or even the possibility of being stoned to death according to Jewish custom. But Mary still chooses to give birth to the Messiah and thereby makes possible the liberation of her people. This courageous action, her risk for life-giving reality, is the beginning of her journey to become a "mature committed woman, growing in her faith in God and the Son."[26]

Indian theologian Astrid Lobo emphasizes Mary's feelings at the annunciation as an Asian woman who wants to make her own choices in her life:

I can feel her fear. Her world is suddenly being turned upside down. God asks her to bear the Son ... and Mary says "yes." It is a "yes" that reverberates throughout her life, as time and time again she is put to the test. ... When Mary makes her choice, human odds are against her. She must have realized that she would probably lose Joseph; that once her pregnancy began to show she would face the possibility of being stoned to death. In her place we would have let common sense prevail, and said, "I'm sorry. Please find someone else." We would forget the one thing that Mary never forgets: the one who asks is God. And so she is willing to pay the price. But the world cannot understand. Not even Joseph. Mary has to be ready to walk alone.[27]

Jesus was born through the body of this woman, "a liberated, mature woman, who had a mind and will of her own, capable of self determination and perseverance in her decisions."[28]

Jesus also did not grow up in a vacuum. Jesus was nurtured and taught by a mother who embodied his people's aspiration for liberation. Asian women theologians claim that Mary announced "what kind of messiah her son will be" through her Magnificat.[29] Mary's vision and life inspired Jesus. Mary's action in the wedding at Cana (John 2) shows that "she is a woman with all the compassionate sensitiveness to other people's needs, often lacking in men, especially those in power."[30] Asian women assume that Mary became an exemplary human being who must have mirrored her humanity to Jesus in the decisive years of his growth. "From first hand experience with his mother,"[31] he was touched by her faith in God, her historical consciousness, and her commitment to her people. Asian women name Mary's teaching to Jesus as "compassionate justice":

It was her [Mary's] openness and receptivity that Jesus showed when he made the blind see, healed the sick and dined with public sinners. It was her unambiguous solidarity with the poor he exercised when he shared their humble and oppressed lot. In his *compassionate justice* he put the good of [hu]mankind above the tyranny of perverted law in the same way she reached out to those who could not help themselves. In his fidelity to the perceived will of the Father, Jesus accepted the consequences of the cross (Jn. 2:1-12) just as she stuck it out with him through her darkest hour of life. Thus, if the scriptural image of Christ shows him to be the model of a new kind of humanity, then it would not be very wrong to say that Mary was his own model.[32]

However, Mary was not always able to understand her son. Mary was rejected by her son. When Jesus was twelve, he said bluntly to his mother who was looking for him with great worry: "Why did you have to look for me? Did you not know that I had to be about my Father's business?" Jesus as a grown man disowned his mother publicly: "Who is my mother?" Mary might have been hurt or humiliated. "Yet she allows him the freedom to be himself."[33] Mary suffered most of her life due to her choice of giving birth to the Messiah. She had to endure ostracized pregnancy, exile, then even her own son's death. She was there when her son was crucified. Many Asian women identify Mary with today's "mothers who suffer as their children are being massacred and taken as political prisoners for their actions on behalf of justice and love."[34]

Mary's great pain and suffering in her life could break neither her spirit nor her faith in God. She refused to be victimized. As an older woman

Mary stayed with the disciples and followers of Jesus, comforting them and holding their shattered dreams after her son's death. Asian women call her "mother of the church," the church "not based on hierarchic domination, but on just relationships."[35] They depict old Mary as a wise, strong woman who gave birth to a new humanity and a new community through her suffering and undefeated hope:

> The woman [Mary] who stands, with other women, at the foot of the cross, and who is present with the community at Pentecost, is an older woman, a woman of wisdom and strength, who suffers, with God, the loss of her son—the consequence of commitment to live for change. It is she who, with the Spirit, gave birth to the Messiah, who makes it possible for the Spirit to give birth to the Church. So, in the home of Mary, Mother of John Mark, Mary becomes the Mother of the new community.[36]

Mary's personal choice to be a mother of Jesus was also a political choice which was connected to the foundation of new community for freedom and wholeness. Her "individual" motherhood was extended to "social" motherhood through her suffering, hope, and revolutionary action.

Mary as Sister: A Woman in Solidarity with Other Women and the Oppressed

Asian women theologians emphasize Mary's solidarity with other women in their writings. They think Mary's visit to Elizabeth shows women's solidarity with other women in the same situation, a development which breaks new ground. Elizabeth also has a scandalous pregnancy because she is pregnant after her biologically fertile years are over. Mary and Elizabeth understand each other since they are brave women of Israel who open their whole beings to the work of the Spirit. They are two sisters who are walking on a new road, risking the safety of a conventional life, due to their commitment to the salvation of Israel.

Mary seeks shelter in Elizabeth's house. "They were a comfort to each other and a source of enlightenment of faith to one another."[37] When women of faith and commitment who are breaking new ground recognize one another's mission in their sisterhood, they overcome their fear of ostracism and annihilation. When they overcome their own fear by supporting one another they can make a bigger move. Their hearts extend to solidarity with all who are struggling to claim their dignity and power as people. Han Kuk Yum of Korea describes this point in her fictionalized Mariology:

> I [Mary] was afraid to meet people's eyes and even Joseph's. However, as soon as I met Elizabeth, my fear suddenly was gone. Elizabeth shouted just when she met me, "Why should this great thing happen to me, my Lord's mother comes to visit me?" "How happy you are to

believe that the Lord's message to you will come true." It will be said this is a spiritual communication. These words of Elizabeth impressed me greatly. I come to realize what great power comes from the understanding and encouragement by a person who is walking the same road. This could be just called sisterhood.

This sisterhood, that takes care of each other, supporting each other is very important for bringing about God's social and institutional change. To accomplish a certain task there should be solidarity of similar-minded people, like the solidarity Elizabeth and I had. So solidarity is an important fact of forming and enriching community. Solidarity, sisterhood does not arise of itself. As Elizabeth, inspired by the Spirit, knew my situation, sisterhood arises from the work of the Spirit. As Elizabeth conceived by God's grace, persons standing in the same situation could and should be joined by bonds of sympathy. In that sense, I would like to have solidarity with all people, especially women who challenge a new possibility. Because women know women's suffering and pain.[38]

When Mary overcomes her fear by being affirmed by her sister in the same struggle, she regains the power to tell the truth. Mary sings a song of revolution, the Magnificat. She expresses her yearning for the liberation of the oppressed people in the words of Hannah—another strong woman of Israel. Mary claims her power and history as a woman whose consciousness is deeply rooted in the heritage and wisdom of the strong women of Israel. Mary makes the forgotten power of her foremother, Hannah, alive by taking action, by accepting the work of the spirit through her pregnancy and by prophesying the "complete change in the present patriarchal order using the words of Hannah."[39] Mary makes connections vertically and horizontally by discovering her foremother and by announcing justice for the oppressed in her own time. Mary's Magnificat is addressed "to an older woman, Elizabeth, who like Hannah, has become pregnant after years of infertility."[40] Elizabeth becomes the first audience for Mary's Magnificat. This shows an important truth: Women need women's presence and affirmation to dare to dream the revolution and to celebrate their power for life.

Mary as a Model for True Discipleship

Asian women see the meaning of true discipleship through Mary. Virginia Fabella asserts that "for too long, Mary has been depicted for us principally as 'virgin' and 'mother'—rarely as 'disciple.' "[41] Fabella emphasizes that Mary's greatness cannot be limited to her motherhood of Jesus. If "a disciple is one who accepts and promotes the teachings of another," Mary should be "the first and exemplary disciple" due to her faith in God and her action. Mary as a young maiden "accepts the challenge of the Holy Spirit at the Annunciation" and "ponders God's word in her heart and responds with courage and determination." She is also "ever ready to be of service to her neighbor" and "is filled with the spirit of prophecy and justice together with the other disciples at Pentecost" while continuing to pray.[42] Mary, then, is not only Jesus' biological mother. She is also a model for true discipleship who has lived her life in faith and has founded the community of faith, the first Christian church. Mary *earns* her place as a mother of the new believing community as a "woman who has heard the Word of God and put it into practice."[43] She receives respect from the community, not because she is a famous man's mother, but because she knows the meaning of "uncertainty and loneliness in the response of faith." She has the priestly power to console the other believers in despair and to nurture the community by uplifting the spirit of the community.

In his final moments, when Jesus says to his disciple, "This is your mother," he does not mean to hand over his elderly mother to others to be taken care of. His words must be understood in the context of his teaching: "Here are my mother and brothers. For whoever does the will of my father in heaven is my brother and sister and mother" (Matt. 12:49-50). Jesus affirms the power and ability of Mary as a head of the family of disciples.

Mary's strength as a disciple lies in her receptive and unbeatable spirit, which enables her to be sensitive to the needs of God and the oppressed people and to refuse victimization in any circumstance. Her receptivity to the spirit of God "does not imply powerlessness nor is it simply a passive trait. Rather, it is a creative submission of a fully liberated human being, who, not being subject to any other human being or human laws, is free to serve God."[44] This receptivity opens her whole life to the prophetic vision and revolutionary action of God and compassion for the oppressed. She is "compassionate and free" to feel the pain of her time and act to change it.[45] Mary represents the meaning of true servanthood.[46] Mary knows what it means to serve God and people and her understanding of servanthood becomes a foundation of the Christian church.

Asian women theologians, however, make it clear that Mary's servanthood is "to God, not to patriarchy."[47] This servanthood is a radical discipleship of discernment, risk, and resistance for liberation, not a passive obedience to the powerful. This radical servanthood of Mary was witnessed in the "people power" of the Philippines, which forced the Marcos regime to collapse in 1987. A Filipino sister, Loretto-Eugenia Mapa, witnessed that the people of the Philippines carried the huge picture and statue of Mary all through their demonstrations in order to sustain their faith and to be empowered by her strength.[48]

Korean Christian women also see Mary's power as a disciple of God and liberation in her unbeatable spirit, which enabled her to move beyond her own personal pain to the founding of a new community of believers. Korean theologian Han Kuk Yum recognizes the analogy between the role of Korean mothers' struggle for grounding democracy and Mary's role as a founder of the new community of the church.[49] Many Korean mothers were among the first to participate in the struggle for democracy because they wanted to protect their children who were arrested, imprisoned, and tortured. But through the process of struggle, they became aware of the broader injustice and evil of military dictatorship and American foreign policy. They realized that the unification and democratization of Korea must be the foundation of a just and safe society. These mothers then joined in the struggle for the unification and democracy of Korea not only for the safety of their children but also out of their own consciousness as responsible Koreans who cared about the destiny of their country.

Like these Korean mothers, Mary nurtured others through her own pain and suffering, and she used this pain and suffering for the foundation of a new human community where equality, justice, and peace would prevail. Her discipleship has become a model for all Christians throughout history who go through pain and suffering but still hope and work to build community for empowerment.

Mary as a Co-Redeemer for Human Salvation

Some Asian women think Mary's role in the salvation of humanity must be recognized as redeemer with Jesus Christ in the Christian tradition. There are two major positions for this claim. One is envisioning Mary as a co-redemptrix by her role as a model for the liberation and salvation of humanity. The other is depicting Mary as a helper and mediator for the redemption of humanity.

The first position is articulated by Emily Mei Ling Cheng. According to Cheng, Mary became a co-redemptrix by her free choice. Mary was first redeemed herself by accepting God's calling as a "co-operator" in the history of redemption. Then she became "our prototype and model" for redemption by showing us our own responsibility for our own cooperation in our redemption.[50] In order to achieve salvation, we, like Mary, have to accept our own redemption freely. Mary shows us that without our cooperation, redemption of humanity is impossible.

The second position is articulated by Loretto-Eugenia Mapa of the Philippines. Mapa claims that "Filipino women's spirituality is very much centered around Mary even to the point that Jesus Christ is obscured."[51] Filipino women think Jesus cannot save the world alone without Mary "because he needs his mother."[52] Mapa traces the origin of this attitude to the pre-Christian, matriarchal indigenous culture of the Philippines. She says that mothers and grandmothers were respected very much by Filipino men and women in pre-colonial culture. This is still true in the Philippines today. Even adult men usually ask their mother's opinion and help when they have to make some important decisions in their lives. Therefore, for Filipinos, Mary is portrayed as a mother who can really help them in their journey for salvation. Filipinos especially worship the "Black Madonna."

Mapa assumes that the wide veneration of the dark-skinned Madonna might be the people's appropriation of the colonial white Mary into their own situation. The Black Madonna might be understood as subconscious resistance against colonialism and affirmation of the dignity of the Filipinos. According to Mapa, Mary became the mother of the poor and works humbly with people, leading people for the struggle for liberation. She is a biblical *anawim* figure. The most holy lady on the pedestal comes down, wears dirty clothing and empowers the poor as one of them. Mapa asserts that "Filipino spirituality can be characterized by the union of the heart of Jesus and the heart of Mary." Mary and Jesus together work for the liberation of the Philippines as co-redeemers.

To summarize, for Asian women Mary symbolizes the birth of a new humanity in their communities and of God's presence in their lives as they struggle against patriarchy in the church and society. What this means for the spiritual life of Asian women is explored in the next chapter.

6

EMERGING ASIAN WOMEN'S SPIRITUALITY

In this world there is no one without ability and there is no one without the right to "win the world." Therefore if women want to attain equality they must first strengthen themselves as individuals. . . .

First, don't allow yourself to become ill. Good health is the most essential thing. Look after it and take tender care of yourself.

Secondly, keep yourself cheerful. . . . Everyday we must do meaningful work, study, contribute something of ourselves to others. Loafing only makes our lives empty, weary and withered.

Thirdly, get into the habit of using your brain. Get rid of your aversion to deep thinking and your strong inclination to always follow the crowd. Think well about what you are about to say or do. . . .

Fourthly, have the determination to drive ahead to the end. . . . Without a great aspiration it is impossible to resist greed and to avoid becoming a victim of comfort. Only those who work for all humankind, not just for themselves, have this kind of aspiration.[1]

What is emerging Asian women's spirituality? Out of their daily struggle for full humanity, Asian women are giving birth to "a spirituality that is particularly women's and specifically Asian."[2] When Asian women gathered together at Singapore in 1987 to articulate an emerging Asian women's theology, they described Asian women's spirituality as:

faith experience based on convictions and beliefs which motivate our thought processes and behavior patterns in our relationships to God and neighbor. Spirituality is the integral wholeness of a person concretizing his/her faith through their daily life experience. Asian women's spirituality is the awakening of the Asian woman's soul to her concrete historical reality—poverty, oppression and suffering. It is a response and commitment of a soul infused by the spirit, to the challenge for human dignity and freedom, and a new life of love.[3]

By defining their own understanding of spirituality, Asian women challenge old notions of spirituality they inherited from the institutional church and conventional religions. They contend that traditional spirituality is "individualistic and removed from the world."[4] It is too concerned about the individual's "interior life of perfection to attain salvation."[5] This kind of spirituality is limited to "one's personal life of prayer and asceticism."[6]

This kind of spirituality is also "removed from the world," largely designed to be practiced by "mystics, monks, priests, and religious, who were said to be 'removed' from the world and its concerns."[7] Asian women believe that this elitist approach to spirituality (largely based on the assumption that only special God-chosen people, who can afford the quiet life of prayer and meditation, have access to the spirit) has made ordinary people passive in their search for spirituality.

Asian women reject this old notion of spirituality and propose a new understanding of spirituality which empowers them. They assert that their new spirituality is "integral, outgoing, community-oriented, active, holistic and all embracing."[8] This new spirituality originates from the concrete life experiences of Asian women. Mary John Mananzan of the Philippines calls this spirituality "gut-level experiences."[9] By this she means a spirituality based on women's "inner-core," her "center" and "heart."[10] Mananzan asserts that "women experience many things but it is their experience as women that touches them most both on the personal and the social level."[11] Out of Asian women's gut-level experience, Asian women's specific spirituality is formulated. We can observe three different moments in Asian women's spiritual formation. These moments, however, are not three linear developmental stages which occur sequentially. Rather, they are like three different rhythms which blend into a spiral dance of Asian women's spiritual formation. The formation of a living spirituality is a continuous process of birth, death, and rebirth. Each of these three rhythms in Asian women's spiritual growth shall now be examined in greater depth.

The Formation of Asian Women's Spirituality

Impasse: Living Death

Asian women's spirituality begins with the reality of impasse. This impasse is caused by their experience of economic, political, cultural, and psychological oppression. Stella Faria of India asserts that Asian feminist spirituality "irrupts through a situation of impasse—suffering pain, poverty, oppression, [and] marginalization."[12] Mananzan describes the situation of impasse as follows:

> As women, we experience regular and everyday discrimination: the limiting experiences of housewives confined to the home, as society assigns them to do; the despair of the wives who are beaten but who cannot separate from their husbands, "because of the children," because of social disapproval or because of emotional and psychological dependance on their husbands. There exist the exploitation, discrimination and sexual harassment of our sisters who work either in the rural areas as invisible contributions to agricultural production or in an urban setting as factory workers. We know about the continuous insult to our womanhood in the mass media, in advertisements and the more blatant exploitation of our sisters in prostitution, mail-order brides, etc.[13]

In these situations, Asian women feel "stuck." Their lives do not grow to the full humanity for which they strive. This feeling of impasse leads Asian women to hate and be ashamed of themselves. The social norms and power structures of their respective cultures and societies make them feel like caged animals. Asian women feel a profound hopelessness, for they do not know of places where they can find help and security. Continuous poverty, political repression, wars, and misogyny produce a despair deep within Asian women.

In addition to the impasse caused by the external structures of oppression, Asian women sometimes also experience chaos in their interior lives. Mananzan calls this "private hells" which are intensified at crisis points in women's lives. Every woman's life is touched by these private hells with much "poignancy and anguish." Mananzan thinks that "from these private hells we emerge either triumphantly with inner liberation or with bitterness and resentment, crushed and mortally wounded in the depths of our being."[14]

In their impasses and private hells, Asian women cry out and struggle in order to find a gate which will lead them to the world of freedom and wholeness. They fight against the various forms of oppressive violence inflicted upon them, keeping them stuck in their impasses and private hells. By stopping their own violence against themselves, the violence of silence, Asian women begin to claim their true selves and take responsibility for their participation in perpetuating the violent system. They are now beginning to refuse to remain silent.

Choice for Life: Discovering True Self

Like an everflowing river journeying from its source to the open sea, Asian women are finding their way out of their impasse by choosing life. This process includes honestly accepting the responsibility for, and control over, our lives. Asian women believe Eve is as responsible as Adam for the Fall. And, like Adam, Eve also "needs repentance and conversion to be accepted into the reign of God."[15] Asian women are especially critical of "the oppression of women by other women" in Asia through the caste and class systems, for example, using other women as domestic servants. They are also concerned about the temptation of accepting tokenism. Asian women believe tokenism will not contribute to the liberation of all women:

> Some women are given a status of equality and privilege as an excuse to perpetuate the general structure and patterns of society. "Token" women are not oriented into the new vision of human relationship and community that the alternative feminist ideology offers: therefore, they are not committed to the work of renewal. Instead they ape the old pattern of individualism and dogged competition for self-glory.[16]

When Asian women begin to become aware of the "false safety" given to them by a social system which keeps women in a socially inferior position, they start to discover their own identity and power. Asian women's "honest admission of shared responsibility in sin, but with hope and faith in the grace of God, which brings wonders and new creation" is the foundation of Asian women's emerging spirituality "that motivate[s] their action and reflection."[17]

To take full responsibility for oneself and to discover and claim one's own identity means to grow into full adulthood. A Burmese woman, Mary Dunn, describes her own awakening to dignified womanhood:

> Before, we Burmese women never felt that we were taken for granted, and oppressed, but now together with our Asian sisters we feel that we are individuals and have our dignity. The first thing that comes to my mind is, we women need to grow upward in spirit, and not be doormats and be downtrodden.[18]

Dunn also says that in the Burmese cultural tradition, which is Buddhist, the husband is "Aing-U-Nat."[19] This means "Chief Spirit" of the house. Wife and children bow down to him twice a day when he goes out for his work and when he goes to bed. Burmese women must respect their husband even if he is cruel to them. In spite of this cultural norm, Mary Dunn discovered that "twenty years of marriage taught me that bearing children and building a perfect home is not enough."

She now thinks women should be "involved in the making of history" by growing beyond their immaturity through affirming themselves and resisting oppression. For her, to be a fully adult woman today means being a woman who can define "who she is and prove what she can do because she has found an identity of her own."[20]

When Asian women experience an "identity of their own," they taste "an inner liberation from the internal and external slaveries."[21] This taste of liberation comes from "their development in self-knowledge, self-acceptance and self-esteem"[22] through their resistance and building a community of wholeness.

Reach Out: Building a Community

Women with "self-knowledge, self-acceptance and self-esteem" have strength to reach out to other people who live under impasse. Asian women think emerging Asian women's spirituality is "lived theology, theology in context," which touches the concrete lives of people.[23] It is "not notions but life itself." They think men have *reasoned* about the true meaning of spirituality throughout history but women have *lived* it. Women's spirituality is a living experience which is different from the abstract concept of spirituality found "in the university desks." Rather, it is something found "in kitchens, laundries, fields and factories." It is "the divine living on grassroot levels."[24]

Since women *live* their spirituality in their everyday lives, they can "feel for others and opt for the needy one."[25] They call it "compassionate spirituality."[26] This compassionate spirituality comes from the "experiences of women giving birth, and caring, and nurturing their children and family."[27] Women give of themselves to others "in order to give life and to provide for others so that all may live."[28] Asian women are critical of the "extreme individualism" they see in Western society. Within the context of Asian women's spirituality, "the self and the community are one."[29]

One Indian Catholic laywoman's spiritual journey vividly illustrates how Asian women develop their spirituality in the midst of Asia's struggle for full humanity. Mercy Mathew is a social worker working with grassroots people in rural India. As a devoted Christian, Mathew wanted since childhood to be a missionary to the poor. But once she had joined a convent for missionary work, she soon was disillusioned. She found there was a vast difference between what she thought a missionary's life would be like and what she actually experienced. She then left the convent and started on her own spiritual journey. Mathew describes what she experienced when she was no longer under the authority and norms of a religious institution but walked alone:

> There was a strange urge to go to these poverty-stricken people yet at the same time there were doubts and confusion because there was no model before me. There was a lack of clarity and direction. . . . This was the beginning of a new chapter in my life. One thing was clear to me — I was not going home to an attractive job or career. I had to be with less privileged people in some sort of humanitarian work. But where? With whom? Doing what? I didn't know. I was uncertain and alone. During this period I experienced rejection and

isolation. I was confronted by many crossroads and I did not know which way to go.[30]

Mathew says this was "an intense period of soul-searching." She visited many places and organizations in order to find the right place to live out her convictions. Finally she found the place where she could feel at peace with herself: a refugee camp. Clarity about her life's direction occurred through her experience in the camp:

> The two years I spent in the Indian and Bangladesh refugee camps were the richest experience I've had in my life. My self-confidence grew and I began to get a clearer picture of the direction my life should take. I decided to go into professional social work.[31]

When Mathew's confidence grew, she saw a clearer picture of the direction of her life because that picture came from within—not outside—herself. As her vision grew so did her strength to reach out and work with the oppressed people in her country. The spiritual growth that accompanied her work came in three phases which she names immersion, activity, and multiplication of oneself.

Mathew makes it clear that working with poor people is not genuinely possible if it is approached with the condescension of a superior person giving charity. Nor is immersion in people's lives just living with them. Instead, it means "declassing" oneself. Mathew had to overcome many temptations to educate, in a patronizing sense, the people with whom she was working. As an alternative, she "sought their help" and looked into herself to give up the "false authority" she had brought from her past intellectual training. The spirit of what Mathew means by immersion is found in the following paragraph:

> Because of my educational background and my past experience there was a tendency to deal with every situation with intellectual superiority. There were temptations to start something visible that would show quick results. It [immersion] meant entering into a new cultural life, too.
>
> I began with my own self, looking into myself, critically reflecting and analyzing, searching, listening and discovering. I had to constantly remind myself that I had no right to go to them as a superior being with a number of do's and don'ts, but be ready to listen to them and to understand them. It also meant involvement in their struggle and the painful breaking up of a number of traditions I had inherited.[32]

When Mathew had learned the power of people's culture and history, she began to take action and organize with villagers for their rights as forest workers against government exploitation. There were many threats from the authorities and some betrayal among the people. But the people continued their struggle. Mathew confessed that she survived the difficulties of the second action phase of spiritual growth because she had "strong faith in the power of the people." She also saw that people "began to grow in confidence and courage" by their action. Once the villagers had won the battle against the government, people from surrounding villages came to visit for advice, legal information, or a chat.

When Mathew's activity reached a peak, she discovered that "the movement had been rather fast" and that she was playing "too active a role." She decided to go into the background. Instead of being an active leader of the community, she "multiplied" herself: the third phase of spiritual growth. By connecting people with literacy, legal, and leadership training organizations, Mathew created an environment and context where the villagers could attain the skills and self-confidence needed for community empowerment. She played many changing roles, primarily defined according to the needs of the community. She is now working with various peoples' organizations and describes her present life with joy: "Life I must say is worth living and I am living it to the fullest."[33]

When she reflects on her life's search and asks, what kept her going, she identifies the reason as her faith in Christ. Jesus' life with the poor and the oppressed has been a continuous source of inspiration for her. Whenever she is in close touch with the oppressed and ill-treated, Mathew finds Christ, both in herself and in the people. She shows us how much we need "inner work" to be truly effective when she shares her own spirituality.

> The need of the time is my maxim. I search for *relevance* and *authenticity*. When I speak of my way of living I mean giving importance to *living*, to *being*. To achieve this a lot of sincere work is needed with the *inner self*. The action then follows. It is innovation. It is a process. It is evolution. I have also learned through this journey that worthwhile things cost and we have to pay the price.[34]

In Mathew's search for life in its fullness is the wisdom of women's spirituality. Mathew overcame her own impasse and confusion by gaining confidence through her work with the poor. She then nurtured the community where all people had the opportunity to also gain confidence and claim their rights and dignity as human beings.

The Characteristics of Asian Women's Spirituality

Asian women name certain characteristics of their emerging spirituality. The following are the main features of their understanding of that spirituality that is specifically "Asian" and "women."

Concrete and Total

Asian women say that their emerging spirituality takes concrete relational reality into consideration. It not only takes women's political and
economic situations seriously but also their cultural and psychological situations. It is "not just a vertical relationship with God but an integral one."
It is shaped "not only by prayer but by relational experience and struggle —
personal, interpersonal, and societal."[35] It is based on the total and concrete
liberation of people (like the exodus) by the people's work with the "God
of history." It is total in the sense that it has something to do with "the
whole person, body and soul in the context of a social milieu." It is concrete
"in the sense of liberation from concrete evils such as injustice, slavery and
exploitation and a working out of concrete blessings like land, posterity,
... etc."[36] There is no place for dualism between body and soul in this
spirituality, because it arises from women's everyday, mundane, bodily
experience.

Creative and Flexible

Asian women think that their spirituality "needs to be creative and flexible" in order to "break patriarchal structures"[37] in the church and society.
They get out of the overwhelming impasses in their lives with genuine
creativity. They make a road out of the wilderness. They break walls when
there is no exit. Asian women's lives have been deprived by so many outer
social forces that they need many inner resources in order to make a way
out when the way is not apparent.

Asian women's spirituality is also flexible. Flexibility is the only way the
victims of oppression can survive under the rigidity of the oppressor's tac-
tics. In their flexible spirituality "faith is not a security in being saved
because of legalistic obedience but is an exciting dimension of radical openness."[38] Asian women do not follow the church's teaching blindly. They
discard the church's teaching if it keeps their lives under bondage. One
example of this is the use of contraceptives. Philippine women question the
interpretation of St. Paul's admonition, "Wives, obey your husbands," when
it comes to the use of women's bodies in the frequency of pregnancy or in
submitting to their husbands every time the latter claim their "marital
right." Mananzan and Lee report on the hidden use of contraceptives
among Philippine women:

> Although the Catholic Chuch has never budged from its insistence on
> the natural method of birth control, about 90 percent of Catholic
> Filipino women quietly contravene this Catholic position and use
> other forms of contraceptives. Not a few have had themselves ligated
> after the birth of their third or fourth child.[39]

When Asian women gain "a clearer self-image" and experience "a process
of inner liberation from the abiding guilt feelings," which were caused by

the church's rigid doctrine and morality, they become more creative and flexible in their appropriation of religious teaching in their daily lives.

Prophetic and Historical

Asian women's spirituality is prophetic in the sense that it seeks "justice and peace for all oppressed and exploited peoples." It "irrupts in history through the concrete life of the poor," and involves "bringing about change in this world." Mary, who sang the revolutionary Magnificat, became an "authentic symbol of spirituality and freedom" for Asian women.[40]

Asian women's prophetic vision is different from that of Asian men because Asian women bring the radical vision of feminism to their spirituality. Feminism promotes radical equality of all human beings. The liberation framework for Asian women brings "a qualitatively different vision and interpersonal relationship from the traditional male ways of constructing communities."[41] The liberative framework of feminism is based on a caring, nurturing, and cooperative model rather than a dominating, conquering, and competitive one.

Community Oriented

Asian women's spirituality is not individualistic. It is always firmly grounded in the community. Manazan and Lee contend that "in the Third World countries, dealing [only] with women's issues cannot uproot all the problems women face in their societies," because Asian women have to overcome the "combinations of political, economic, and religio-cultural oppressions within the underlying patriarchal domination."[42]

In order to achieve their liberation, Asian women have to fight against many different forms of oppression. These include national struggles against colonialism and neo-colonialism and the people's struggle against military dictatorship. The struggle includes women, men, children, and all oppressed people for whom salvation is "communal," not "private."[43] Building a community where all live the fullness of life in harmony is the ultimate goal of Asian women's spirituality.

Pro-Life[44]

Asian women's spirituality comes from "their concrete pro-life way of living and experience."[45] No matter what their racial, class, ideological, and religious backgrounds, women have not been known for destroying the lives of their children in order to defend their "isms." Men kill their own and other people's children in the name of abstract causes through wars. In a male-dominated society, women's pro-life spirituality is trivialized as cowardly, myopic, and lacking historical consciousness. Asian women believe that the "disastrous dimension of patriarchal culture is typically exemplified in its demeaning, ignoring, and despising the very spirituality of women that is oriented toward and sustaining life in love."[46]

One powerful example of women's pro-life spirituality, which transcends the rigidity of "isms," comes from Sri Lanka. Sri Lankan Christian woman activist Anita Nesiah describes women's non-violent resistance against racism and militarization of the country. Many attempts have been made over the last ten years to solve the violent conflict between the Singhalese-dominated national government and the Tamil minority. Even though there were "pacts between political leaders, multi-party conferences, a presidential commission, legislative changes, an international peace accord, and various types of military action," peace was not established in Sri Lanka.[47] Nesiah contends that the men in her country failed to keep the peace and suggests an alternative model of fostering peace. She proposes that women of both groups mount a united front against violence "by adopting non-violent methods such as *satyagraha* (truth force) and *ahimsa* (love) developed by Mahatma Gandhi."[48]

According to Nesiah, "there is striking similarity between [the] military and the patriarchal family." Both are based on the assumption of *obedience*: the lower positions in the hierarchy must obey the higher. The commander is synonymous with the father figure. Therefore, "the image of ideal soldier and the image of ideal mother are almost similiar." Both have to sacrifice "for the structure where they belong." The only difference between soldier and mother is the former is sacrificing his life in order to take another person's life while the latter is sacrificing in order to give life to others.[49]

Nesiah believes in women's ability for *satyagraha* and *ahimsa* because women know what it means to give birth to others and thus to value life. Nesiah describes how Sri Lankan women from the North (Tamil) and Sri Lankan women from the South (Singhalese) supported each other in their non-violent resistance to keep the peace in Sri Lanka. Mothers from both sides joined together for prayer, fasting, and action. She says, "Maybe non-violence is not practical but it is prophetic."[50] Nesiah believes women's endurance, weeping, and non-violent action will contribute to weaving the tapestry of peace in her country.

Ecumenical, All Embracing

In Asia, where Christians are less than 3 percent of the population, "interfaith dialogue is an important part of the discussion of emerging Asian women's spirituality."[51] They reject Christian triumphalism, "which is the spirituality of colonialism and neo-colonialism."[52] They are searching for ecumenical spirituality, "which seeks unity of humankind in humility and reverence toward all life and all belief systems."[53] Ecumenical spirituality is not based on doctrinal exchanges. Rather it is based on "radically new values that are people oriented, concerned for life and for a truly humane community."[54] Asian women insist that "the core of emerging women's spirituality [is the] search for the wholeness of life."[55] Different religions meet one another in their common search for this wholeness.

Many Asian women have lived an *ecumenical spirituality* long before the term was articulated by scholars. Asian women draw sacred sources into their lives in order to survive their difficult life situations. Filipino women, for example, worship *Ina* ("divine mother" in Tagalog) in the form of the Virgin Mary. When they pray to Mary, mother of Jesus, they call her *Ina*. Originally *Ina* came from Filipino folk religions. *Ina* was the source of life, a deeply revered goddess. When Spanish colonizers evangelized Filipinos to Catholic Christianity, Filipinos transformed the Mary of their colonizers into the indigenous *Ina*.[56] In the Philippines, as elsewhere in Asia, women have chosen life-giving religious symbols beyond the narrow doctrines and norms of the institutional church. The poorer and closer Asian women are to grassroots culture, the freer they appear in changing religious symbols of the dominating group for their own needs.

Another example of truly ecumenical spirituality is found in the story of a Korean mother who fought against the powerful with her spiritual wisdom and won. According to this story, a politician ran over and killed a boy with his car. The accident was clearly the fault of the politician, but he refused to take responsibility for it. Since he had much power with the police in the city, he managed to avoid blame.

Some time later the politician ran for Congress. The slain boy's grandmother felt so angry that she made and distributed leaflets charging the politician with his crime at his nominating convention. The politician responded by suing the grandmother for libel; the powerless grandmother lost the case because of a corrupt trial and was imprisoned.

In anger and despair the boy's mother responded by creating her own path of revenge. She drew portraits of the politician, police chief, judge, and politician's lawyer. Every morning in front of a bowl of pure water, she prayed for justice to the deities she knew: *Ha-neu-Nim*, *Kwan-Woon-Chang-Nim*, and *Ye-Su-Nim*.[57] After prayer, the boy's mother shot each portrait with a bow and arrow. The rumor of her prayer and action spread all over the city. The men who had hurt her became very frightened; in the Korean shamanistic tradition, the boy's mother's ritual would lead to the men's deaths. In order to stop this spiritual energy directed against them, the men released the grandmother from prison and financially compensated the family for the boy's death.[58]

In this powerless mother's story is seen a glimpse of Asian women's ecumenical spirituality. In this case of extreme anger and helplessness, the Korean mother draws on all the survival resources around her. She asked for help from the supreme Korean god, a god from the shamanistic tradition, and from Jesus. Doctrinal purity or religious boundaries were not of concern for her. What mattered was the life-giving power of justice in whatever forms it comes. True ecumenism is possible when each religion liberates the oppressed out of their bondage.

Cosmic, Creation-Centered

Asian women claim that their spirituality emphasizes the cosmic dimension.[59] Asian women's spirituality is not limited to human beings but also embraces the whole cosmos: animals, plants, water, the earth, air, and the rest of the universe. Asian women assert, then, that their emerging spirituality "draws its vitality from creation as contrasted with the traditional spirituality that focuses on the fall and redemption."[60] It is a creation-centered spirituality. It is a spirituality that celebrates life and the goodness of creation. It is a spirituality that is "joyful rather than austere, active rather than passive, expansive rather than limiting."[61]

In this spirituality God does not appear as a cruel judge. Instead, God is the "One who united," is both "masculine" and "feminine" and both "Eastern" and "Western." Jesus also has a very liberating portrait in that he is seen as "a prophet and an artist." The human individual "has transcended the dualistic body and soul relationship and has [an] optimistic view of the possibilities of personhood."[62]

Cosmic, creation-centered spirituality is often seen in the folk religions or popular religiosity in Asia. One good example is the worship of the divine mother (*Ina*) in the Philippines.[63] According to Consolacion Alaras, an important characteristic of the covenant is "the image of the Mother as the Divine Womb—a source of life and nurture—which protects and seeks only that which engenders and sustains the life of all its parts," which includes men, women, animals, the earth, and all other living things.[64] The Divine Mother is "not the ruler of the world" but she is "the world itself." She is the "Great Goddess" who is immanent in nature. When the world itself becomes the goddess, "the respect for the sacredness of all living things [follows] automatically."[65] This Divine Mother, who has been transposed with Mary, the mother of Jesus, has been worshiped widely among many people in the Philippines.

The Diverse Manifestations of Emerging Asian Women's Spirituality

Asian women confront day-to-day impasses in their lives with their spirituality, and affirm the goodness of life in spite of the multilayered oppression they face. This everyday struggle to survive is the most powerful manifestation of emerging Asian women's spirituality. It is important to note the collective dimensions of Asian women's spirituality in order to honor their effort to put their energies together for social change.

There are three prominent features in the collective manifestations of emerging Asian women's spirituality. These are: 1) the flowering of women's consciousness-raising groups; 2) the growing women's movement within the context of the people's liberation movement; and 3) the sharpening of women's intellectual reflections within the Asian context.

In many countries in Asia women are joining in small groups and intimately sharing their life stories. There are groups of "artists, poets, spiritual dancers," and women who are "involved in women's health and family planning."[66] There are also groups from women workers' unions, women farmers' unions, and women slum-dweller organizations. When these women speak the truth of their lives in a small-group setting, they are empowered by other women's support and move away from self-hate, shame, and guilt. They achieve a clearer understanding of their authentic selves, which have been obscured by patriarchy. These Asian women also form a "collective consciousness," which leads them to struggle against exploitation and discrimination. Sometimes divorced women and single mothers are "learning to face life alone, conquering their emotional and psychological dependency, finding meaning in life apart from their estranged male partners."[67] At other times, "women among the urban poor and in labor unions [achieve the] sense of sisterly solidarity" that strengthens them in their movement for justice.[68]

The emergence of strong women's movements in Asia is another powerful manifestation of Asian women's spirituality. Asian women say, "Following Jesus is not alone a private route, but is a collective enterprise."[69] Asian women join together in solidarity within the wider context of the people's movement to fight for their survival right. In most Asian countries women cannot separate their struggle as women from the national struggle as Third World people. They fight for the betterment of all people through the process of claiming their rights as women.

The sharpening of women's intellectual reflections is also a powerful aspect of Asian women's spirituality. They begin to exercise women's intellectual critique of the religious, cultural, political, and economic teachings and theories of their respective dominant cultures. Asian women discover that women are "very often excluded even by the ideology of wholeness and holistic salvation."[70] They believe that "patriarchy can never be holistic."[71]

> Patriarchy is basically androcentric, and it can never include women and children in the center of its world as equals. Even love for women and children is for men's own selfish needs. That is the reason why women and children are put perpetually on the periphery even if mechanisms of make-believe are woven into their emotional and financial dependency.[72]

Asian women in religious circles think that to discriminate against women in the name of respect for traditional cultures and religions is no longer acceptable no matter how beautiful those cultures and religions' original meaning.

On the one hand, Asian women are confronted with "rediscovering their history and are resurrecting their women leaders, heroines, and saints of their particular tradition as sources of cooperation and strength for their struggle."[73] Examples of this are the enshrinement of "Princess Urduja and Gabriela Silang" in the Philippines and the honoring of "Mira Bai, Panditta Rama Bai" in India. Asian women are searching for women honoring empowering resources "in their own traditions, myths, and legends" in order to achieve "the full flowering of their womanhood."[74]

On the other hand, Asian women are undertaking a critique of culture and religion. They participate in the interfaith dialogue "sorting out what are the really liberating elements and what are the oppressive elements in them."[75] Through this sharp cultural and religious analysis, Asian women are looking for either alternatives or a new synthesis of religio-cultural understanding where women's lives are honored. In this sense Asian women's theology is one of the most important manifestations of their emerging spirituality.

"Emerging Spirituality of Asian Women," woven together by Mananzan and Lee, gives an excellent statement on the emerging spirituality of Asian women:

> It celebrates rather than fasts, it surrenders rather than controls. It is an Easter rather than a Good Friday spirituality. It is creative rather than conservative. . . . Spirituality is a process. It is not achieved once and for all. It does not become congealed. It is not even a smooth, continuous growth. There can be retrogression or quantum leaps. It has peaks and abysses. It has its agonies and its ecstasies. The emerging spirituality of women promises to be vibrant, liberating, and colorful. Its direction and tendencies seem to open up to greater possibilities of life and freedom, and therefore to more and more opportunities to be truly, intensely, and wholly alive![76]

7

The Contribution and the Future of Asian Women's Theology

The preceding chapters examined the historical context of emerging Asian women's theology and its reflections on humanity, Jesus, Mary, and spirituality. This final chapter will summarize and identify the contribution of Asian women's theologies based on women's struggle for self-determination and for full humanity in Asia, and will also offer some comments about the future of Asian women's theology.

A New Understanding of Theology

Even though Asian women's experience of the divine is ancient, their naming of Christian theology as *Third World*, *Asian*, and *Women* is recent. Their journey toward the new naming of God has just begun. The roads Asian women take are diverse; their experiences of the journey are also diverse. God has many names and Asian women's naming of God takes many forms and colors. We can observe, however, four prevalent images of theology which are growing among Asian Christian women.

Theology as "Cry, Plea, and Invocation"

Asian women's theology is "a cry, a plea, and an invocation" to God. It is a sound of *han* bursting out from women's despair and impasse. It is their tearful yearning for God's justice when there is no justice in Asian women's lives. It is also their prayer for God's healing presence in this war-making, people-killing, and nature-destroying world. Asian women's theology may not have an adequate systematic structure or the proper academic terminology in the traditional sense, but it arises out of women's experience of encountering God in their gut, feeling God in their heart, and communicating with God in their soul. Kwok Pui-lan of Hong Kong expresses this point:

You ask me what shape feminist theology in Asia will take. Will it start with "beyond God the Father" and finish with "beginning from the other end?" Will it be coloured by the rhetoric of middle-class elites or heavily laden with socialist terminology? Will it yield a systematic analysis of the situation of women in Asia or just an emotional outburst like that of a lunatic?

For these questions, I have no answer. I only know that feminist theology in Asia will be a cry, a plea and an invocation. It emerges from the wounds that hurt, the scars that do not disappear, the stories that have no ending. Feminist theology in Asia is not written with a pen, it is inscribed on the hearts of many who feel the pain, and yet dare to hope.[1]

If women's theology in Asia "is not written with a pen" but "is inscribed on the hearts" of many women who "feel the pain, and yet dare to hope," theology can no longer remain in the hands of a few intellectual elites who have academic training in traditional theology. Theology must become democratized. Since all conscious experience is already interpreted experience, Asian women's experience of the divine already has its own theological interpretation. Their cry, plea, and invocation to God is a powerful interpretation of God's presence in our midst. This democratized theology is people's theology, popular theology, and folk theology, which works in people's everyday lives.

Theology as "God-Praxis"

Asian women's theology is *live-ing* theology. For Asian women theology is not just talking or thinking about God; it is living the liberation and wholeness here and now. According to Elizabeth Tapia of the Philippines, "Human liberation, not God talk, is the primary focus of theology."[2] While evaluating Filipino women's emerging theology, she gives a new name to theology. Tapia calls theology "God-praxis" rather than "God-talk."

Theology is not only a theoretical exercise. It is a commitment and participation in people's struggle for full humanity, and discernment of God's redemptive action in history. It is theology-in-action.[3]

Tapia's definition of theology as God-praxis, then, is different from that of male liberation theologians who advocate the definition of theology as the "second step."[4] In Tapia's definition of theology there is no dualism or sequential order between action and reflection. A "commitment and participation in people's struggle for full humanity" and "discernment of God's redemptive action in history" are an integral whole. One does not precede the other. The Asian woman's life itself, her reflective action and engaged reflection together, are God-praxis, living theology in Asia.

Theology as Embodied, Critical Reflection

Asian women's emphasis on the democratization of theology by all people with all kinds of life experiences, however, does not undermine the importance of critical reflection in their theologizing. Asian women realize that they need well-developed, analytical frameworks with which they can see the nature of the interconnections of the many different oppressions around them. In recent years theologically trained Asian women have put their energies into articulating the meaning of Asian patriarchy and Asian women's hermeneutical principles.[5] Asian women theologians have found that they need to define their own theology in relation to the traditional theologies of their oppressors in order to name the evil of the oppressors' theology as clearly as possible and also to claim their right for the full humanity manifest in the gospel of Jesus Christ. Asian women, therefore, are training themselves to develop their ability for critical reflection through formal and informal theological education, bible studies, women's conferences, and participation in the women's and people's movements. They are learning how to do social and biblical analyses and are making connections between their oppression in society and their religious experience. Their analyses and critical reflections are based on their "lived-world experience." Therefore, Asian women's theology as critical, embodied reflection avoids "the violence of abstraction."[6]

Theology as "Vision Quest" [7]

Asian women's theology includes more than Asian women's immediate expression of their experience of God, their praxis, and critical analysis in their concrete historical situation. Their theology is also their vision quest. Asian women are yearning for the "community of the harmonious life on the earth," where people "regain the image of God," and where "all kinds of animals and [hu]mankind together live in harmony"[8] and "they shall not hurt or destroy" (Isa. 11:6-9).

For Asian women, theology is a language of hope, dreams, and poetry. It is firmly based on concrete, historical reality but points to the mystery and vision that calls Asian women from the future and the depth of all that is. The power of this vision and mystery carries Asian women through their *han* and impasse. It enables them to keep moving, flowing with the rhythm of the universe even when the heartbeat of the universe seems to be destroyed by human greed and hatred. Theology as a language of hope, dreams and poetry is not a luxury for Asian women. It is an active healing power in the midst of despair. Theology as vision quest is not an escapist, otherworldly addiction of the oppressed. It is remembering the original wholeness of creation and activating the dangerous memory of the future.

A New Understanding of the Identity of Theologians

Who are the theologians in emerging Asian women's theology? If Asian women's theology is people's theology and popular theology, then every

Asian woman who believes in and reflects upon the meaning of the goodness of creation, the radical egalitarian values of Jesus Christ, and the
coming of God's justice in her midst — and tries to live out that reality — is
a theologian. Asian women have expressed their theology through their
prayers, songs, dances, devotional rituals, drawings, and the way they live
in the community. They are the theologians who are carving out oral theology and non-verbal theology from body languages. The majority of such
women have not received formal theological training from traditional educational institutions.

Only a few Asian women have articulated their theology through writing.
This written theology among Asian women was begun only during the last
decade. Most Asian women who write and publish theologies in Asia today
have had some kind of traditional theological training, are of middle-class
background (by origin or educational status), and have been exposed to
Western feminist theologies. Many Asian women theologians write their
theology in English. Most of the theologies included in this book have come
from such women. These middle-class, educated, and English-speaking
women talk about Asian women's pain — poverty, physical and psychological
battering, prostitution, and so on. They talk about poor women's suffering
in Asia. But what right do they have to talk about poor Asian women's
struggles? How can they speak of the poor Asian women's faith with
authenticity using the language of their colonizers, which the poor women
in their respective countries cannot even understand? What is the relationship between the educated middle-class women theologians who *write*
theology and the illiterate, poor women theologians who *live* theology in
their everyday lives?

This is a great problem for Asian women theologians. It is discussed
often as they seek to overcome their separation from their poor sisters. It
is not an alienation easy to overcome; it is perhaps a lifetime struggle. What
is important for our study is that Asian, Western-educated women have
identified this problem and are fighting to bridge the gulf between them
and their sisters. Asian middle-class women have identified *solidarity* with
poor women as the goal of their struggle.

Many educated women theologians in Asia know that they are not doing
theology *for* the poor women. They articulate theology in order to enhance
the liberation process in their broken communities, seeking the common
future of the communities. These women do theology as a form of repentance and self-criticism. They also do theology in order to become more
critically aware of their privilege and their responsibility in relation to the
poor women in their communities. These middle-class, educated Asian
women theologians are learning how to work with poor women and how to
be transformed by the wisdom of the poor through the process of doing
theology. Asian women theologians know that this process of *metanoia* to
poor women is the only way to regain their wholeness.

Elizabeth Tapia describes what it means to be a Western-educated, Filipino religious scholar who wants to be accountable to the poor Filipino women's struggle for liberation and full humanity. While Tapia is fully aware of the contradictions in "being an Asian woman student in the West with its problems and privileges," of being a religious scholar in a country whose interventionist policy hurts her people, she shares her intention of doing theology:

> I am approaching this study [her research on Filipina women's the-ology] from the perspective of a Filipina Christian committed to the promotion of Third World people's struggle for justice and full humanity. . . . Now, as a church worker and student of theology, I feel committed to work with the poor, learn from them and be affected by them. Am I attempting to write a theology for the poor Asian women or for the women of the Philippines? No. It is my desire to be in dialogue with them while learning from them, as I have done in the past. When appropriate, I want to lift their concerns and echo their voices.[9]

Tapia wants her theology to become an echo for poor Filipino women by lifting their concerns when appropriate. Tapia wants the silenced voices of poor Filipino women to be heard by her becoming an echo of their cries. By echoing their cries, Tapia is participating in the struggle of Filipino women. Echoes do not change the original sounds; echoes resound the original sounds. In this sense such echoes are the most honest and powerful testimony to the poor woman's voice of truth when the "culture of silence" suppresses women's truth-telling with various political, economic, and social devices which destroy any coherent sound from women. This image of echo will be the vital image for the educated, middle-class women doing theology in solidarity with poor women in Asia until that time when the echo changes into a symphony in which every woman, regardless of background, with the fullness of her humanity, is able to make her own sound of truth heard.[10]

Asian women have begun to break the silence by becoming an echo to one another. Through their interactions in the women's movement, nation-alist movements, and movements against poverty and political oppression, women hear one another's stories, fight for their common survival and liberation, and build a sustainable community. Their theology comes out in the process of building humane communities. When there is genuine shar-ing, hearing, and naming for the survival and liberation of the community, *then the community becomes the theologian.* Through building just and har-monious communities, which include women, children, and men, Asian women live the God-praxis.

A New Methodology

Asian women's approach to the creation of theology, like all other forms of liberation theology in the Third World, is *inductive*, drawn from experience and commitment. It is also *collective* in its approach and *inclusive* in its perspective and goal.[11]

This inductive, collective, and inclusive methodology creates a distinctive *Asian women* flavor in their theology. During the last decade women in several Asian countries conducted many Asian women's theological consultations. Many of these consultations followed the method proposed by the Women's Committee of EATWOT. The EATWOT method has its circular steps: listening to individual's situations, social analysis, and then theological analysis.

It starts with women's *storytelling*. Women from various backgrounds gather and listen to one another's stories of victimization and liberation. Educated middle-class women theologians are committed to inviting or visiting poor farmers, factory workers, slum-dwellers, dowry victims, and prostitutes and listening to their life stories. Storytelling has been women's way of inheriting truth in many Asian countries because the written, literary world has belonged to privileged males. Until the turn of the century many Asian families did not teach girls how to read and write. Women sustained their truth, which was distorted by the definitions of the male literary world, by telling stories mouth to mouth. The power of storytelling lies in its *embodied truth*. Women talked about their concrete, historical life experience and not about abstract, metaphysical concepts. Women's truth was generated by their *epistemology from the broken body*. Women's bodies are the most sensitive receiver for historical reality. Their bodies record what has happened in their lives. Their bodies remember what it is like to be a *no-body* and what it is like to be a *some-body*.

Korean minjung theologian Kim Young Bok, who as a male minjung theologian feels deep solidarity with women's struggle in Korea, proposes a theological methodology based on storytelling for *han*-ridden Korean women and other oppressed people. He and Korean women theologians want to form bridges between minjung theology and Korean women's theology. Kim calls this storytelling methodology *socio-biography*.[12] According to Kim, women's socio-biography shows an understanding of history which cannot be perceived by so-called objective social analysis. Women's socio-biography brings out the "hidden reality" behind official sociological and historical documents. Listeners of socio-biography hear not cold data but actual people's suffering, crying, and longing. This encounter with foremothers and contemporary sisters in struggle through their storytelling touches Asian women's hearts. It motivates Asian women to participate in the people's struggle for liberation because the people in the stories are real people who tremble with fear and yearn for the touch of their beloved.

When Korean women theologians, for example, hear a poor, old Korean woman's life story, they hear the recent history of Korea. Through her story they learn what it means to be colonized and sexually abused by the Japanese, and what it means to lose a husband during the Korean war (a war caused by a cruel international power struggle). Korean women theologians perceive the current complex political, economic, social, and cultural history of their country when this old woman unfolds her story about a son who is a poor farmer exploited by a dictatorial government, her grandson who works for very low wages in a factory owned by an American and Japanese multinational corporation, and her granddaughter who sells her body to foreigners for financial survival. It is an embodied historiography. Poor women's socio-biography is "holistic, multidimensional and complex,"[13] because it deals with the whole person and not some single aspect of personhood. It is more than a detached witness against sexism. It includes colonialism, neo-colonialism, cultural imperialism, racism, classism, and the evils of patriarchy. When women hear other women's stories, they cry, experience anger, and console one another. The boundaries between storyteller and listener become softened. Listeners feel the oppressed women's pain deeply; their hearts are touched and transformed when other hearts reach out for healing on the personal and political level.

I have had the privilege of sharing moments of deep connection with other women by listening to their stories. I participated in the EATWOT Asian women's consultation held in Manila in 1985. Small groups of Asian women theologians visited farming and fishing communities and also visited women workers at a picket line. Their stories of pain, courage, and determination empowered our commitment for justice for our own people. The most painful moment I experienced was visiting several prostitutes at one of the infamous red-light districts in Manila with two other Asian women theologians. Since we did not want to take these young women's precious working time, we paid for the seats, drinks, and fees for hiring hostesses as the men did.[14] We sat with three prostitutes at a corner of the bar and listened to their stories: why and how they came here, what their daily lives are like, what their struggles and hopes are. Two of the young prostitutes told us this was their first night. They were nervous and afraid of what would happen to them. The third, who had been working in this bar for several months, expressed empathy toward the newcomers and comforted them.

All three women came from poor farming families and had first tried to find jobs as factory workers and housemaids. They were unable to find such work because of the high rate of unemployment in the Philippines. Other jobs simply were not available to them. These three women shared with us their guilt, shame, and anger about their situation, the society which permitted this to happen to them, and men. As Catholics, they wanted to get out of their situations but did not know where to go or how to survive without prostitution. Each of the prostitutes shared how she felt about the church and Christianity; the women knew our work and why we wanted to hear about their struggle. They said they were very ashamed of themselves because they sinned every day. They also said they were never able to talk about their pain and guilt to parish priests in confession because they knew the priests would condemn their mortal sin and tell them to stop prosti-

tuting themselves immediately, without providing any alternatives for survival. We Asian women theologians recognized and were angered by the
truth of our prostitute sisters' statements, including the hypocrisy of the
church. We felt in our guts that the same patriarchal, capitalist system
which forced our sisters into prostitution binds all Asian women with the
potential of a similar fate. To see and listen to the dehumanization and
"de-womanization" of these young prostitutes caused our eyes to overflow
with tears. Even though I and my fellow Asian women theologians could
not take these young women out of prostitution, we all became more determined to create a theology which is accountable to them. By exposing the
evil and sin of patriarchal capitalism (in this case manifested by these young
prostitutes' desperate oppression through international sex-tourism) and
offering a theological alternative, we Asian women theologians hope our
work will empower the liberation process of these and all our struggling
Asian sisters.

This method of active listening to women's storytelling, especially those
from the bottom stratum of Asian society, is one of the most important
parts of Asian women's theologizing; it leads Asian women theologians to
critical social analysis. Their social analysis includes political, economic, and
religio-cultural analysis. If storytelling and listening to women's socio-biography gives Asian women theologians the inspiration and courage for revolutionary change, then critical social analysis gives them a chance to see
with clarity the whole picture of complex interconnections in the evil structure. Sometimes Asian women theologians create social analysis by themselves; other times they include women with professional training in
sociology, economics, or political science. Asian women theologians scru-
tinize the ways capitalism, patriarchy, militarism, and religio-cultural ideologies work together to escalate the degree of women's oppression. They
use many new insights from women's studies, counter-colonialist historical
studies, critical sociologies, and nationalistic leftist ideologies from the
Third World people's movement.

With the questions and new awareness coming from critical social analysis, Asian women theologians move to *theological reflection*. They approach
the Bible as part of their theological analysis. Asian women do not start
from biblical teachings about what humans or society should be in order to
understand their reality. Instead, Asian women theologians start from their
own historical situation and ask what relevant teachings the Bible has to
the questions they have, such as land reform, private property, the meaning
of work, poverty, and sexual exploitation. Yet Asian women know the
"Bible cannot solve their problem in a concrete way"[15] because there is a
great cultural and historical gap between the period the Bible was written
and the present reality. Asian women theologians use the Bible as a *reference* and an insight from which they draw wisdom for their lives, and not
as an absolute unchangeable truth from God.

The theological voice of Kwok Pui-lan of Hong Kong represents the views of many Asian women theologians on the Bible. Kwok is fully aware of the role the Bible played to perpetuate "Western domination" and "cultural imperialism" in Asia.[16] She claims missionaries' emphasis on the absolute truth of the Bible over Asian culture put truth from the Asian religious cultural tradition in an inferior position to the truth of Christianity. Kwok strongly objects to this missionary point of view of the Bible. Furthermore, she "reject[s] both the sacrality of the text and the canon as a guarantee of truth." Kwok also thinks the Bible does not provide the norm for interpretation in and of itself. She explains why such a "mystified" view on the Bible is dangerous for oppressed people, and she encourages a new way of understanding the Bible:

> For a long time, such "mystified" doctrine has taken away the power from women, the poor and the powerless, for it helps to sustain the notion that the "divine presence" is located somewhere else and not in ourselves. Today, we must claim back the power to look at the Bible with our own eyes and to stress that divine immanence is within us, not in something sealed off and handed down from almost two thousand years ago.[17]

Holding the immanent view on truth, Kwok suggests "dialogical imagination" as an alternative way of interpreting the biblical truth from Asian women's perspective. It is dialogical because "Asian Christians are heir to both the Biblical story and to our own story as Asian people, and we are concerned to bring the two in dialogue with one another."[18] It is also imaginative "for it [dialogical imagination] looks at both the Bible and our own Asian reality anew, challenging the established 'order of things.' "[19]

Through dialogical imagination Asian women discover from both bible stories and their people's stories the wisdom needed for their own survival and liberation. It is a critical process which enables Asian women to choose good news rather than bad news from the Bible. Asian women theologians want to free the Bible and its interpretation from its age-old captivity by patriarchy, colonialism, and Western cultural imperialism. With all the insights Asian women theologians have discovered from women's stories, social analysis, and biblical reflection, they critically review from their own perspectives the traditional doctrines of Christian theology in anthropology, Christology, Mariology, ecclesiology, and pneumatology. Asian women theologians also reflect on the theological meanings of the urgent issues around them such as sex-tourism. Korean women theologians call this latter part of their methodology *hyun jang* theology.

Hyun jang is translated as the place where historical events are happening. *Hyun jang* theology evolves around the concrete issues Korean women confront in their everyday lives. The Korean Association of Women Theologians organized a *hyun jang* theology group after their second consultation for the establishment of feminist theology in Asia in October 1984.

This consultation was the first consultation where Korean women theologians used the three-step EATWOT method of theological reflection discussed earlier in this chapter. Many women who participated in the consultation were touched deeply by the storytelling of oppressed women in Korean society. Seminary-trained middle-class women, who make up the majority of KAWT's members, reevaluated their theology in light of what they heard from these poor women. KAWT members confessed that they had not felt much genuine solidarity with the poor women of Korea and repented their sin of ignorance in the final statement of the consultation:

> Until now we have been ignorant and unconcerned about our neighbors who suffer, are exploited and oppressed at the bottom and fringes of our society. Therefore, we confess that our theology must start with repentance.[20]

KAWT members became determined to create a theology directly connected with the everyday concrete life struggles of Korea's poor. The *hyun jang* theology group was the outcome of KAWT's commitment to be accountable to poor Korean women. KAWT has theologized on the women workers' fight against their exploitative factory owners at the Sung Do corporation; on the Korean women's movement against the early retirement policy in many companies;[21] on police torture of women college students.[22] Korean women theologians have joined the struggle of women not only in their theologizing but also on the picket line. As a consequence, the general secretary of KAWT, Ahn Sang Nim, was arrested by the police and spent time in a police jail.[23] Korean women theologians are learning about the cost of discipleship in their solidarity with other Korean women in *hyun jang*.

According to the new methodology which has developed from Asian women's theological struggle, the most important *source* of theologizing is lived-world experience. This is *women's* specific experience, which cannot be universalized the way some traditional, bourgeois European male theologians have standardized *common* human experience. The specific historical experience of Asian women is manifested in their struggle as victims and agents of liberation as women. Asian women also use their religio-cultural and socio-political traditions for theologizing. They claim their identity as both Asian and Christian. They take themselves seriously. Asian women have begun to appropriate life-giving living traditions into their theology while rejecting male-defined or imperialist traditions which hinder Asian women's growth to full humanity.

Recently Asian women theologians have started to look into Asian myth, folktales, songs, poems, proverbs, and religious teachings from Hinduism, Buddhism, Islam, Taoism, shamanism, tribal religions, Confucianism, and Christianity for their theological resources. They also have begun to discover the work of women revolutionaries, freedom fighters, and radical thinkers from our historical past. Asian women are inspired by their fore-mothers' courage, wisdom, political ideologies, and alternative vision for a new society. This process has helped Asian women theologians see how patriarchal traditions inherited to them from so-called normative theological sources are inadequate and oppressive.

Asian women theologians also accept scripture as a theological source. They use the Old and New Testaments along with other teachings from Asian traditional religions. They selectively choose liberating messages from the text in light of their *hyun jang*. They also expose patriarchal evil by illustrating the oppressive messages from the texts. Asian women theologians learn from texts but go beyond them to meet the community. In this sense they liberate the texts.

Asian women use all the above sources with critical consciousness. Critical consciousness is different from so-called neutral, detached, and objective reason. Critical consciousness is an engaged subjective reason which takes sides. Critical consciousness is the thinking power which uncovers the ideology of domination.

Throughout the metamorphosis of the new naming of God, Asian women have formulated a norm which will lead them to the core of truth. Korean theologian Lee Oo Chung echoes many Asian women's voices:

> What is the norm for women's theology? That must be something which can contribute to recovering of women's full humanity and all other oppressed people. The norm should be something to do with how it will empower the oppressed victims to stand again as precious children of God.[24]

To paraphrase Lee, the norm for Asian women's theology lies in its liberating power, which frees women from the many layers of oppression. Its transforming power heals Asian women to wholeness and enables them to celebrate their lives in fullness with other oppressed people in their communities.

The Future of Asian Women's Theology

This final section suggests the future direction of Asian women's theology and sums up the emerging insights of Asian women. I want to share my conviction on the future of Asian women's theology as one of the *second-generation liberation theologians*. By second-generation liberation theologians, I mean the younger generation of liberation theologians who have built their theology upon the foundation of the *first-generation liberation theologians* but then moved beyond them. The first generation mainly reacted against the colonial legacy; the second generation theologians have been able to move beyond reaction toward the construction of their own positive theological reality.

Many of my generation's teachers were trained in Europe or North America and spent most of their energy attempting to understand the spiritual reality of our people through Western theological concepts and symbols which do not touch the hearts of our people. Some of the Western-oriented Asian theologians claimed to be liberation theologians. To this day some still use Western theological formulas inherited from the missionary tradition in order to react against the colonialist tendency among Western theologies. These Asian theologians point out the cultural imperialism of Western theologies and maintain that a radical break is needed with the West in order to produce authentic Asian theology. Their work, however, has not yet produced the needed break or an adequate Asian theology.

Some Asian theologians have used Asian resources for their theology, but the heavy Christocentrism in their work prevented them from being transformed by the religious wisdom of the poor of Asia. The majority of the poor in Asia are non-Christian and thus experience their ultimate reality through non-Christian idioms and symbols. Out of the first-generation liberationists' arduous struggle, we second-generation theologians were born. We owe much to our teachers because they gave us "master's tools" and the space to create.

Second-generation liberation theologians are deeply aware of the neo-colonial power surrounding us, but we also know our own power. We know what we are for and we construct our own life-giving works. We believe in our experiences and no longer must give power to outside authorities. We start our theology from owning our own gut feelings and experiences. We know from our painful history that the most dangerous thing for an oppressed people is to become numbed by internalizing alien criteria and denying our gut feelings. If we do not permit ourselves to fully experience who we are, we will not have the power to fight back and create our own space. We have to touch something real among and around us in order to meet God. Unlike the first-generation liberation theologians in Asia, we of the second generation do not spend our energy reacting mainly against the colonial legacy. We now spend our energies naming our experience with our own terms and creating theological alternatives that are liberative for us.

The future of Asian women's theology must be understood in the context of this struggle. Since Asian women have been systematically alienated from theological education due to the patriarchal domination of the church and society, many Asian women who are doing theology have carved out their own theological niche and have developed their own voice. They do not use prescribed theological formulas; instead, they derive their authority from the principle of the "hermeneutical privilege of the poor." Since these Asian women theologians are poor in terms of traditional theological education, they are freer from academic and doctrinal authority. Asian churches and seminaries have never taken women seriously as theologians who have the ability to articulate their faith. The attitude of these institutions is, "Why bother? They are only emotional women anyway." This neglect was ironically a disguised blessing for women theologians. For women created their own alternative spaces to gather together, as in bible study groups and prayer meetings, to develop their theologies. New rituals have been practiced and spread among women in Asia without being noticed by the institutional church.

Honoring the legacy of those Asian sisters who were the active agents of symbol-making, I will make four theological suggestions for the future of Asian women's theology. First, Asian women theologians should realize that *we are the text*, and the Bible and tradition of the Christian church are the context of our theology. Asian churches have given so much authority to the Bible and Christian tradition of the West that our peoples' stories have become insignificant. Under the influence of the missionary fundamentalist churches the Bible was regarded as the complete and final revelation of God's truth. It, therefore, became the norm through which our peoples' lives were validated. The underlying reality was that the Western missionary's interpretation of the Bible became the yardstick to measure the truth of our people's experience. This ahistorical view of the Bible and Christian tradition has perpetuated the cultural dependency of Asian Christians upon the so-called Mother Church in the West.

Of course we Asian Christians must open ourselves to learn from the authentic collective memories of Jewish and Christian people in the West, but not to the degree that the latter become the totalitarian dictators in our world of spiritual meaning. The Bible becomes meaningful only when it touches our peoples' hearts, especially women's hearts that have been deeply wounded by the patriarchal teachings of the Bible. The Bible becomes a transforming power in our peoples' struggle for self-determination and wholeness only when biblical stories of liberation are reenacted in our peoples' daily lives. Then, and only then, the Bible becomes a living book for us. The authentic memories of God's people were not completed two thousand years ago, and they cannot be imprisoned within the Christian canon. The text of God's revelation was, is, and will be written in our bodies and our peoples' everyday struggle for survival and liberation. God did not come first to Asian women when Western missionaries brought the Bible to Asia. God has always been with us throughout our history, long before Jesus was born. The location of God's revelation is our life itself. Our life is our text, and the Bible and church tradition are the context which sometimes becomes the reference for our own ongoing search for God. We should unfold the ever-growing truth of God in history as the text of God's revelation through our lives.

My second hope for the future of Asian women's theology is that we shift our theological focus from institutionalized religion to *popular religiosity* among women. Almost all institutional religions of Asia have been founded and dominated by men. Women have been excluded from the process of institutional religions. Male-defined institutional religions have always been oppressive to Asian women in many parts of their teachings. Men have distorted the meaning of womanhood by projecting their fear and hate to women throughout history.

Male religious leaders, however, could not succeed in domesticating or destroying Asian women's spirit completely. Asian women have revolted. They have kept the life-giving faith of their mothers, grandmothers, and great-grandmothers in their kitchens, wells, fields, and mountains. On the surface Asian women look as though they are obeying the teachings of their male religious leaders, but underneath their docile appearances they have the subversive power to transform the abstract, misogynist, institutional religions into women-affirming, body-loving, and nature-honoring spirituality. I call this spiritual practice women's popular religiosity. The existence of women-defined popular religiosity in Asia, such as Korean shamanism, folk Chinese Buddhism which venerates Kwan In (female goddess), Filipino worship of Ina (mother-God), is powerful evidence of women's resistance to patriarchal religions.

In general, Asian women's popular religiosity could be called cosmic religion, which revolves around the rhythm of the cosmos, the here and now on the earth. Their religiosity is different from meta-cosmic religions, which are mainly represented by male-dominating, so-called higher world religions. Meta-cosmic religions always try to go beyond this material world in order to find the purer forms of spiritual reality. Many male scholars in religion view meta-cosmic religion as a higher form (more evolved) than cosmic religion. They often call cosmic religion primitive, just as patriarchal society defines women as inferior to men. These male scholars perceive cosmic religion as something to be domesticated or directed by meta-cosmic religion in order to be moral and historical. This idea likewise mirrors how women are perceived in patriarchal society: immoral and thus in need of male domination.[25]

Women-centered cosmic religion has been *the religion from the underside of religion* in patriarchal culture. Many such religions were actively persecuted by governments and institutional religions. They are, however, the only religious space where women's leadership is respected as sacred. In this space Asian women have carried out distinctive women's spirituality, which dances with the cosmic rhythm of the universe, not against it. This is the time for Asian women to rediscover the wisdom of our foremothers' life-giving popular religiosity in order to survive on Mother Earth, which is increasingly threatened by rapist-type technology and nuclear war.

My third hope for the future of Asian women's theology is that it go beyond accepting religious pluralism through interreligious dialogue toward *religious solidarity* and also toward revolutionary praxis in the peoples' struggle for liberation. To recognize the plurality in diverse manifestations of the divine is important in order to fight the fascist, imperialist mentality that fosters exclusivity of one's own claim to truth. Acceptance of plurality, however, is not enough for Asian women's theological future because an understanding of pluralism does not necessarily and automatically lead Asian Christian women to the liberation struggle of other Asian sisters who come from different religious, class, and racial backgrounds. Pluralism easily becomes lazy and irresponsible when it cannot mobilize women from many backgrounds toward common, concrete historical projects.

Asian women's theologies (at least written ones) still have the tendency to be dominated by middle-class, Western-educated English-speaking women who do theology in order to *understand* the world. Asian women's theology must become a revolutionary praxis that empowers other Asian women to *change* the unjust socio-political and religio-cultural structures so that we may all live with the radical power of mutuality in this world.

My fourth and last hope for the future direction of Asian women's theology is that it move away from the doctrinal purity of Christian theology and risk *the survival-liberation centered syncretism*. In their struggle for survival and liberation in this unjust, women-hating world, poor Asian women have approached many different religious sources for sustenance and empowerment. What matters for them is not doctrinal orthodoxy. Male leaders of the institutional church always seem preoccupied with the doctrinal purity of their religions. What matters to Asian women is survival and the liberation of themselves and their communities. What matters for them is not Jesus, Sakyamumi, Mohammed, Confucius, Kwan In, or Ina, but rather the life force which empowers them to claim their humanity. Asian women selectively have chosen life-giving elements of their culture and religions and have woven new patterns of religious meaning.

Syncretism has been such a "dangerous" word for Western theologians. They believe syncretism destroys Christian identity and will eventually lead people to confusion. Syncretism, for them, is the lazy and irresponsible way of combining different religious heritages without any principles.[26] They talk as if Christian identity is an unchangeable property which they own. Any radical break of Asian theologians from orthodoxy in an effort to dive deep into our Eastern traditions and be transformed by them has been considered suspicious by Western church leaders. Traditional Western theologians seem to say to us that they have the *copyright* on Christianity: "All rights reserved—no part of our teaching may be reproduced in any form without our permission."

We Asian women theologians must move away from our imposed fear of losing Christian identity, in the opinion of the mainline theological circles, and instead risk that we might be transformed by the religious wisdom of our own people. We may find that to the extent that we are willing to lose our old identity, we will be transformed into truly *Asian* Christians. We have to ask tough questions of the mainline Christian churches and seminaries and also of ourselves. Who *owns* Christianity? Is Christianity unchangeable? What makes Christianity Christian? How far can we make ourselves vulnerable in order to be both truly Asian and truly Christian?

I do not know what kind of new spirituality and theology will come out of Asian women's struggle to be authentically who we are in the fullest sense. I do know, however, that the future of Asian women's spirituality and theology must move away from Christo-centrism and toward life-centrism. We Asian women no longer are passive soil for the Christian seed of truth (the imagery so often used to describe Christian missions in Asia). Rather, we will be mothers who will actively participate in the birth of the new spirituality and theology which will carry our specifically Asian, Third World, and women's genes. We are expecting an arrival of a new spirituality and a new theology which will empower poor Asian women in their "struggle to be the sun again."

NOTES

Introduction

1. See Audrey Lorde, *Sister Outsider* (New York: The Crossing Press, 1984), p. 110.

2. For information on the term "hermeneutics of suspicion," see Juan Luis Segundo, *The Liberation of Theology* (Maryknoll, New York: Orbis Books, 1976); José Míguez Bonino, *Doing Theology in a Revolutionary Situation* (Philadelphia: Fortress Press, 1975).

3. For a resource on Korean women's lives under Confucianism, see Lee Ock Kyung, "A Study on Formational Condition and Settlement Mechanism of *Jeong Juel* (Faithfulness to Husband by Wife) Ideology of Yi Dynasty," Master's thesis, Ewha Women's University, 1985.

4. See Paulo Freire, *Pedagogy of the Oppressed*, trans. Myra Bergman Ramos (New York: Seabury Press, 1970).

5. Lorde, p. 41.

6. Nantawan Boonprasat Lewis, "Asian Women Theology: A Historical and Theological Analysis," *East Asian Journal of Theology* 4:2 (October, 1986), p. 18.

7. See Kwok Pui-lan, "Chinese Women and Christianity 1860-1929," Ph.D. diss., Harvard Divinity School, 1989.

8. See Elizabeth Tapia, "The Contribution of Philippine Christian Women to Asian Women's Theology," Ph.D. diss., Claremont Graduate School, 1989.

9. See Marianne Katoppo, *Compassionate and Free: An Asian Women's Theology* (Maryknoll, New York: Orbis Books, 1980).

10. See Park Soon Kyung, *Minjok Tongil Kwa Keedokyo* [*Unification of the Nation and Christianity*] (Seoul, Korea: Hankilsa, 1986).

11. See Park Soon Kyung, *Hankook Minjok Kwa Yeosung Shinhak eu Kwajae* [*The Korean Nation and the Task of Women's Theology*] (Seoul, Korea: Daehan Keedokyo Suhwhe, 1983).

12. See Virginia Fabella and Mercy Amba Oduyoye, eds., *With Passion and Compassion* (Maryknoll, New York: Orbis Books, 1988).

13. See Mary John Mananzan, ed., *Essays on Women* (Manila: St. Scholastica's College, 1987).

14. See Mary John Mananzan, ed., *Women and Religion* (Manila: St. Scholastica's College, 1988).

15. See The Centre for Society and Religion, ed., *A Hymn to Creation: Essays in Women and Religion* (Colombo, Sri Lanka: The Centre for Society and Religion, 1983).

16. See The Centre for Society and Religion, ed., *God, Women and the Bible* (Colombo, Sri Lanka: The Centre for Society and Religion, 1983).

17. See Aruna Gnanadason, ed., *Toward a Theology of Humanhood: Women's Perspective* (Delhi: All India Council of Christian Women, 1986).

18. See Korean Association of Women Theologians, ed., *The Context of Korean Women's Theology* (Seoul, Korea: KAWT, 1983).

19. See Korean Association of Women Theologians ed., *The Task of Korean Women's Theology* (Seoul, Korea: KAWT, 1983).

20. See Christian Conference of Asia, ed., *Reading the Bible as Asian Women* (Singapore: CCA, 1986).

21. See Virginia Fabella and Lee Sun Ai, eds., *We Dare To Dream: Doing Theology as Asian Women* (Seoul, Korea: Asian Women's Resource Center, 1989; Maryknoll, New York: Orbis Books, 1990).

22. See *CTC Bulletin* 4:3 (December 1983).

23. See *East Asia Journal of Theology* 4:2 (1986).

24. Lewis, pp. 18-22.

25. The names of interviewees are Lee Oo Chung, Cho Wha Soon, Lee Sun Ai, Chung Sook Ja, Kang Myung Soon, and Sohn Eun Ha from Korea; Aruna Gnanadason from India; Marlene Perera and Bernadeen Silva from Sri Lanka; Elizabeth Tapia, Loretto-Eugenia Mapa, and Virginia Fabella from the Philippines; Kwok Pui-lan from Hong Kong; and Nantawan Boonprasat Lewis from Thailand.

26. The names of these interviewees are Hyun Young Hak, Ahn Byung Mu, Suh Kwang Sun, Kim Yong Bok, and Park Sang Jung from Korea; Tissa Balasuriya, Aloysius Pieris, and Preman Niles from Sri Lanka; M. M. Thomas, Samuel Rayan and K. C. Abraham from India; Yeow Choo Lak from Singapore; James Cone from the United States; and Mercy Amba Oduyoye from Ghana.

1. The Historical Context

1. For examples of this area of study, see Joanna Liddle and Rama Joshi, *Daughters of Independence: Gender, Caste and Class in India* (Delhi: Kali for Women, 1986); Kumari Jayawardena, *Feminism and Nationalism in the Third World* (Delhi: Kali for Women, 1986).

2. I have witnessed many abuses of Asian church women by the glorification of suffering in their churches. One member of the Asian Women Theologians' Group, for example, who did not identify herself to protect her privacy, shared her experiences of suffering in marriage. She said her ex-husband, who was a leader of the Catholic Worker's movement and a devout Christian, commanded her to suffer if she wanted his love. He said to her, "You are not worthy of my love since you have not suffered for me for more than twenty years like my mother. You have suffered for me only for two years!" The Asian woman who shared this story told me her ex-husband's words to her were the same as those read in a prayer each day in the Catholic Mass. The prayer starts with "I am not worthy of your love, Lord." She made a connection between suffering and love in her marriage and church life. In her church to be a good Christian was to suffer, just as the way to be a good wife in her marriage was to suffer. I know other examples of the glorification of suffering in Christian women's lives in my own church experience and through many other Asian women's sharings.

3. M. M. Thomas, "Some Notes on a Christian Interpretation of Nationalism in Asia," *South Asian Journal of Theology* 2:2 (1960), p. 26.

4. See North East Asia Theological Education Educators' Conference, Seoul, Korea, *Theological Education and Ministry Report* (Taiwan: The Presbyterian Bookroom, November 28-December 2, 1966), p. 19.

5. See Gerald H. Anderson, ed., *Asian Voices in Christian Theology* (Maryknoll, New York: Orbis Books, 1976); Douglas J. Elwood, ed., *Asian Christian Theology: Emerging Themes* (Philadelphia: Westminster, 1980); Emerito P. Nacpil and Douglas J. Elwood, eds., *The Human and the Holy: Asian Perspectives in Christian Theology*, (Maryknoll, New York: Orbis Books, 1978).

6. Tapia, p. 42.

7. Ibid., p. 43.

8. Ibid., p. 41.

9. See CCA Women's Concerns Committee, *Reading the Bible as Asian Women* (Singapore: CCA, 1986).

10. See CCA Women's Concerns Committee, *Women to Women: Asian Women in Solidarity: Mobilizing Women in Struggles for Food, Justice and Freedom* (Singapore: CCA, 1986).

11. Ibid., p. 1

12. The accounts of the EATWOT meetings have been published. For the Ghana meeting, see Kofi Appiah-Kubi and Sergio Torres, eds., *African Theology En Route* (Maryknoll, New York: Orbis Books, 1979); for the Sri Lanka meeting, see Virginia Fabella, ed., *Asia's Struggle for Full Humanity* (Maryknoll, New York: Orbis Books, 1980); for the Brazil meeting, see Sergio Torres and John Eagelson, eds., *The Challenge of Basic Christian Communities* (Maryknoll, New York: Orbis Books, 1981); for the India meeting, see Virginia Fabella and Sergio Torres, eds., *Irruption of the Third World: Challenge to Theology* (Maryknoll, New York: Orbis Books, 1983); for the Geneva meeting, see Virginia Fabella and Sergio Torres, eds., *Doing Theology in a Divided World* (Maryknoll, New York: Orbis Books, 1985). For an excellent brief history of EATWOT, see James H. Cone, "Ecumenical Association of Third World Theologians," *Ecumenical Trends* 14:8 (September 1985), pp. 119–22.

13. Fabella shared with other Asian women theologians at the EATWOT Conference in New Delhi, December 1987, that: "The male liberation theologians thought that I deserved to serve them but I did not deserve to go to the conference."

14. Appiah-Kubi and Torres, p. 194.

15. See Fabella, *Asia's Struggle for Full Humanity*.

16. Ibid.

17. Rose Zoe-Obinga, "From Accra to Wennappuwa: What Is New? What More?" in Fabella, *Asia's Struggle for Full Humanity*, p. 175.

18. See Cora Ferro's article, "The Latin American Woman: The Praxis and Theology of Liberation" in Torres and Eagelson, pp. 24–31.

19. Torres and Eagelson, p. 28.

20. Fabella and Torres, *Irruption of the Third World*, p. 248.

21. Ibid., p. 249.

22. Ibid., p. 200. Emphasis mine.

23. Fabella and Torres, *Doing Theology in a Divided World*, p. xvi. Emphasis mine.

24. Ibid., p. 186.

25. Fabella and Torres, *Irruption of the Third World*, p. 205.

26. Fabella and Oduyoye. The book is an account of the meeting.

27. Mananzan, "Theology From the Point of View of Asian Women," p. 2.

28. I attended the consultation as an observer. I was invited as a representative of Asian Women Theologians (AWT), a support group for Asian women and Asian-American women who are studying and doing theology in the United States.

29. See *Proceedings: Asian Women's Consultation.*

30. Lee Sun Ai, interview with author, Inter-Church Center, New York City, August 9, 1988. Lee shared her personal struggle as a theologically trained Asian woman who wanted to contribute to the larger society but was rejected in many church-related organizations because she was a woman. She also described how she started *In God's Image.*

31. Marianne Katoppo, "Editorial," *In God's Image* (December 1982), p. 3. (Hereafter *In God's Image* will be referred to as *IGI*.)

32. Original members of the committee include Lee Sun Ai; Barbara Stephens, Education Secretary, CCA; Karen Campbell-Nelson, United Church Board for World Ministries; and Maria Goh, Secretary to the Department of Communication, CCA.

33. "Introduction," *IGI* (December 1982).

34. Ibid.

35. Ibid.

36. The advisory committee consists of Virginia Fabella from the Philippines; Marianne Katoppo from Indonesia; Lee Oo Chung from Korea; Matsui Yayori from Japan; Barbara Stephens from New Zealand; and Jessie B. Tellis Nayak from India.

37. Funds have been raised for the center, now located in Seoul, Korea.

2. The Social Context

1. For a new understanding of God among Asia women, see *IGI* (September 1988), especially "My Image of God" by Astrid Lobo.

2. "Womanity" was used by Asian women theologians at the EATWOT Asian Women's Consultation in 1987 in order to emphasize women's full humanity, which was distinctive from male-defined universal humanity.

3. Kwok Pui-lan, "God Weeps with Our Pain" in *New Eyes for Reading: Biblical and Theological Reflections by Women from the Third World*, ed. John S. Pobee and Barbel von Wartenberg-Potter (Geneva: World Council of Churches, 1986; Oak Park, Illinois: Meyer Stone Books, 1987), p. 90.

4. Asian Women's Consultation, "Highlights of the Asian Women's Consultation" in *Proceedings: Asian Women's Consultation* (Manila: EATWOT, 1985) p. 3.

5. Sohn Duck Soo, *The Research on Poor Women in Korea* (Seoul, Korea: Minjing Sa, 1983), pp. 85–86. Translation mine.

6. Virginia Fabella, "Asian Women and Christology," *IGI* (September 1987), p. 14.

7. Ibid.

8. Aloysius Pieris, *An Asian Theology of Liberation* (Maryknoll, New York: Orbis Books, 1988), p. 87.

9. Padma Gallup, "Doing Theology—An Asian Feminist Perspective," *CTC Bulletin* 4:3 (Singapore: CCA, December 1983), p. 22.

10. For the documentation of these criticisms in Asia, see Kamla Bhasin and Nighat Said Khan, *Some Questions on Feminism and Its Relevance in South Asia* (Delhi: Kali for Women, 1986).

11. For Asian women's witness to this experience, see Lee Sun Ai "The Women's Movement and the Ecumenical Agenda," in *Weaving New Patterns*, ed. Jennie Clarke (Hong Kong: World Student Christian Federation, Asia/Pacific Region, 1986), p. 65.

12. Bhasin and Khan, p. 2.

13. Ibid.

14. Ibid., p. 4.

15. For examples, see Bhasin and Khan, p. 17.

16. Ibid., p. 14.

17. For more information on the Korean women workers' struggle, and on Cho Wha Soon, who was an active participant in the movement, see *Let the Weak Be Strong: A Woman's Struggle for Justice*, ed. Lee Sun Ai and Ahn Sang Nim (Oak Park, Illinois: Meyer-Stone Books, 1988).

18. Cho Wha Soon, interview with author, New York, May 1986.

19. Ibid.

20. Park No Hai, "Darning a Bed Sheet," trans. Lee Sun Ai, *IGI* (April 1985), p. 3.

21. Ibid.

22. In Korea, people honor women's dreams right before or after their pregnancies. We believe that this dream prophesizes the future of babies. Dragon dreams have been considered good fortune for the baby. Dog dreams do not have much significance for the future of the baby.

23. *Our Story*, translation mine (Seoul, Korea: Hand printed by a workers' collective, n.d.), pp. 63-64.

24. "A Discussion on Feminism," *Asian Women* 11:36 (September 1986), p. 1.

25. Bhasin and Khan, p. 14.

26. See Edward W. Said, *Orientalism* (New York: Vintage Books, 1978).

27. Quoted in "Backstreet Guides to Degrading Slavery," *CCA News* 23:1/2 (January/February 1988), p. 13.

28. This comment comes from a black woman student who participated in James Cone's course on "Black Theology" at Union Theological Seminary in New York City during the spring semester of 1985.

3. Struggle To Be the Sun Again

1. This song was written by Nargis Basu, a well-known Indian poet. See Clarke, pp. 108-10.

2. For more information, see Marie Mignon Mascarenhas, "Female Infanticide and Foeticide in India" in *Stree* 16 (October 1987), pp. 14-15. *Stree* is an occasional newsletter of the All India Council of Christian Women.

3. For an excellent presentation on Asian women's situation, see *Balai* 2:4 (December 1981).

4. "Final Statement: Asian Church Women Speak" (Manila, Philippines, November 21-30, 1985) in Fabella and Oduyoye, p. 119.

5. From a Sri Lankan liturgy presented at an Asian women theologians' conference in Manila in November 1985. *IGI* (March 1987), p. 7.

6. Aruna Gnanadason, "Women's Oppression: A Sinful Situation," in Fabella and Oduyoye, p. 73.

7. Ibid.

8. Ibid.

9. "Report of Indonesian Theologically Trained Women's Consultation" (Sukabumi, June 24-29, 1983), *IGI* (December 1984), p. 9.

10. Lee Oo Chung, "Korean Traditional Culture and Feminist Theology," in *The Task of Korean Feminist Theology* (Seoul, Korea: Korean Association of Women Theologians, 1983), p. 77.

11. Sixty-six women and men, drawn from various churches in India, attended the National Consultation on "Towards a Theology of Humanhood: Women's Perspective," November 21-24, 1984, Whitefield, Bangalore. This ecumenical consultation was organized by the All India Council of Christian Women (Women's Subgroup of the National Council of Churches in India), Catholic Women, and the Association of Theologically Trained Women in India. The consultation was sponsored by EATWOT as a part of establishing Asian women's theology. The findings of the consultation were published in book form by the All India Council of Christian Women. For more information see, Gnanadason, *Towards a Theology of Humanhood*.

12. "Liturgy Used at the Indian Women Theologians' Conference," in *IGI* (December 1984), p. 28.

13. *Minjung* is a Korean word meaning "people," specifically "oppressed people." According to a Korean minjung theologian, Suh Kwang Sun, minjung are "the oppressed, exploited, dominated, discriminated against, alienated, and suppressed politically, economically, socially, culturally, and intellectually, like women, ethnic groups, the poor, workers and farmers, including intellectuals themselves." (From Suh Kwang Sun's class lecture given at the School of Theology at Claremont Graduate School, August 1983.) The term *minjung*, therefore, is a bigger and broader concept than *proletariat*. Minjung theologians try to articulate theology out of the concrete historical experience of the Korean minjung.

14. Hyun Young Hak, "Minjung: The Suffering Servant and Hope," a lecture given at James Memorial Chapel, Union Theological Seminary, New York, April 13, 1982, p. 2.

15. See Suh Nam Dong, "Toward a Theology of *Han*," in *Minjung Theology* (Maryknoll, New York: Orbis Books, 1983), pp. 55-72.

16. Ibid.

17. Lee Oo Chung, pp. 63-78.

18. Ibid., p. 67.

19. Ibid., pp. 74-75.

20. Ibid., p. 74.

21. For more information on the Asian women's movement, see *IGI* (April 1986).

22. Sigrid, "Through Woman's Eyes," *IGI* (December 1985/February 1986), pp. 31-32.

23. See Lee Sun Ai, "A Reading from a Taoist Funeral Song Designated for Women," *IGI* (April 1984), p. 5.

24. Lucy D'Souza, "My Sadhana," *IGI* (September 1988), p. 18.

25. Rita Monterio, "My Image of God," *IGI* (September 1988), p. 35.

26. Jurgette Honclada, "Notes on Women and Christianity in the Philippines," *IGI* (October 1985), p. 17.

27. Susan Joseph, "I Am a Woman," *IGI* (September 1988), pp. 30-31.

28. Her prostitute support group, called *Han-so-ri* ("the sound of *han*" or "big sound"), was in the Yong San area in Seoul, Korea. This group was enabled by Maryknoll sisters from the United States. These Catholic sisters did not impose their religion on the prostitutes, nor did they try to evangelize Korean prostitutes into Christianity. What the sisters did was offer sanctuary to the prostitutes. I visited them in the summer of 1987 and had an opportunity to share some time with the prostitutes.

29. Interview with the author, Seoul, Korea, August 10, 1982.

30. This consultation was held during May 24-27, 1983. The issue of homosexuality was debated among participants of a bible study led by Old Testament scholar Dr. Elizabeth G. Dominguez.

31. Consultation report from Theologically Trained Women of the Philippines, "A Continuing Challenge for Women's Ministry." *IGI* (August 1983), p. 8. (Hereafter referred to as "A Continuous Challenge.")

32. Ibid.

33. *IGI* carried an article, "Emerging Patterns in the Women's Movement in Asia," in its December 1985/February 1986 issue in which associate editor Ranjini Rebera interviewed seven feminist women from different Asian countries on their involvement with the women's movement in their respective countries and the women's movement's relationship to church and society. Interviewees were: Ruth Kao (Taiwan), Audrey Rebera (Sri Lanka), Jocelyn Armstrong (New Zealand), Saramma Jacob (India), Prakai Nantawasee (Thailand), Cynthia Lam (Hong Kong) and Andrea McAdam (Australia).

34. A poem by Akiko Yosano from Japan. It is believed that this poem was written in the dawn of the century. In *Voices of Women: An Asian Anthology*, ed. Alison O'Grady (Singapore: Asian Christian Women's Conference, 1978), p. 13.

35. Gallup, p. 22.

36. Ibid.

37. Ibid.

38. Chitra Fernando, "Towards a Theology Related to a Full Humanity," *IGI* (April 1985), p. 21.

39. Virginia Fabella, "Mission of Women in the Church in Asia: Role and Position," *IGI* (December 1985/February 1986), p. 8.

40. "A Continuing Challenge," p. 7.

41. Ibid.

42. Ibid.

43. Monteiro, p. 35.

44. Ibid.

45. Lee Sun Ai, "Images of God," *IGI* (September 1988), p. 36.

46. This phrase has been chosen as the World Council of Churches' mission goal for the next decade. Many Asian church women welcome this direction and have had national consultations in order to carry out this goal.

47. Susan Joseph, "Images of God," *IGI* (September 1988), p. 37.

48. Lee Sun Ai, "Images of God," p. 37.

49. Astrid Lobo, "My Image of God," *IGI* (September 1988), p. 38.

50. Ibid.

51. Pearl Derego, et al., "The Exodus Story," *IGI* (September 1988), p. 48.

52. Fernando, p. 24.

53. Hiratsuka Raicho, "The Hidden Sun," in O'Grady, p. 10.

4. Who Is Jesus for Asian Women?

1. "Summary Statement from the Theological Study Group," paper presented at the Consultation on Asian Women's Theology on Christology, Singapore, November 20-29, 1987. This consultation was sponsored by *In God's Image*. For more information on the conference, see *IGI* (December 1987-March 1988). The documents from the consultation were published in *IGI* during 1988-1989. (Hereafter referred to as Consultation on Asian Women's Theology–1987.)

2. Ibid., p. 1.

3. Ibid., p. 2.

4. Ibid.

5. Choi Man Ja, "Feminist Christology," Consultation on Asian Women's Theology—1987, p. 3.

6. Komol Arayapraatep, "Christology," Consultation on Asian Women's Theology—1987, p. 6.

7. This is the common teaching Asian women receive from the institutional, male-dominated churches in Asia. When I was a Sunday school teacher at a Korean church in Orange County, California, in 1983, I witnessed a Korean woman, who was a bible teacher for a college student group, share her experience of death and resurrection of self in front of the entire congregation. She confessed how sinful she was in relation to her husband. She said that she was not able to obey her husband because she thought he was not reasonable and fair. So she argued with him a lot. One day her husband, who was a medical doctor, threw a kitchen knife at her out of anger during an argument. Fortunately the knife missed her and stuck into the wall behind her. At that point, she said, she experienced the love of God through the judgment of her husband. She believed then that as a wife she had to obey her husband as God's will. She witnessed to the congregation that her old self was *dead* and her new self was born through her husband's *love*. This woman concluded her statement with: "There have been no arguments and only peace in my family after I nailed myself on the cross and followed God's will." After her talk, the entire congregation responded to her with a very loud "Hallelujah!" This is only one example of "woman hate" in Asian churches. I have heard countless examples of women's oppression in the church from other Asian women through various church women's gatherings.

8. For more information on the missionary history of China, see Kwok Pui-lan, "The Emergence of Asian Feminist Consciousness on Culture and Theology" (Hong Kong: unpublished paper, 1988).

9. I know that there are conflicting views on the role of the missionaries in Asia. Some people think that their role was destructive and others believe it was positive. My view is that their role was primarily, though not exclusively, negative.

10. Lydia Lascano, "Women and the Christ Event," in *Proceedings: Asian Women's Consultation* (Manila: EATWOT, 1985), pp. 121-29.

11. Ibid., p. 123.

12. Ibid., p. 125.

13. Ibid.

14. Virginia Fabella, "Asian Women and Christology," *IGI* (September 1987), p. 15.

15. Choi, p. 6.

16. Ibid.

17. Park Soon Kyung, Hankook Minjok Kwa Yeosung shinhak eu Kwajae [*The Korean Nation and the Task of Women's Theology*], p. 50.

18. See Honclada, pp. 13-19.

19. See Mary John Mananzan, "The Philipino Woman: Before and After the Spanish Conquest of the Philippines," in *Essays on Women*, pp. 7-36.

20. Ibid.

21. Park Soon Kyung, Hankook Minjok Kwa Yeosung Shinhak eu Kwajae [*The Korean Nation and the Task of Women's Theology*], p. 47.

22. Ibid.

23. Ibid., p. 48.

24. Ibid.

25. Ibid., p. 49.

26. Ibid., p. 47.

27. Consultation on Asian Women's Theology—1987, p. 2.

28. Monica Melanchton, "Christology and Women," Consultation on Asian Women's Theology—1987.

29. Ibid., p. 1.

30. Ibid.

31. Ibid., p. 2.

32. Ibid., p. 4.

33. Ibid., p. 6. Note the contradictory theological position on the appropriation of the Hindu notion of God in Christian theology (cf. Gallup).

34. Lee Oo Chung, "Korean Cultural and Feminist Theology," *IGI* (September 1987), p. 36.

35. Ibid.

36. Ibid., p. 37.

37. Ibid.

38. Ibid.

39. Ibid., p. 38.

40. Ibid.

41. "Women and the Christ Event," in *Proceedings: Asian Women's Consultation* (Manila: EATWOT, 1985), p. 131.

42. Ibid.

43. Pauline Hensman, "Women and the Christ Event," in *Proceedings: Asian Women's Consultation* (Manila: EATWOT, 1985), p. 116.

44. Lascano, p. 121.

45. Ibid., p. 125.

46. Ibid., p. 127.

47. Ibid.

48. Ibid., p. 128.

49. Ibid.

50. Ibid.

51. Kwok, "God Weeps with Our Pain," in Pobee and von Wartenberg-Potter, p. 92.

52. Lee Oo Chung, "One Woman's Confession of Faith," in Pobee and von Wartenberg-Potter, p. 19.

53. Ibid.

54. Ibid.

55. Ibid., pp. 19-20.

56. Ibid., p. 20.

57. Ibid.

58. Marianne Katoppo, "Mother Jesus," in O'Grady, p. 12.

59. Katoppo, *Compassionate and Free*, p. 79.

60. Katoppo, "Mother Jesus," in O'Grady, p. 12.

61. Park Soon Kyung, *The Korean Nation and the Task of Women's Theology*, p. 51. See also James Cone, *God of the Oppressed* (New York: Harper and Row, 1975). Cone makes a similar argument. For Cone, Jesus is black because if Jesus represents

oppressed humanity, Jesus must be black in our historical situation where black people are constantly crucified.

62. Choi, p. 8.

63. Ibid., p. 7.

64. Ibid., p. 6.

65. See Virginia Fabella, "Asian Women and Christology."

66. Ibid.

67. Ibid.

68. Gabriele Dietrich is of German origin. Since 1972 she has been working in South India, first in Bangalore, and for the last ten years in Madurai, teaching in a Tamil-medium college. She is committed to the women's movement. I include her as a theologian in India due to her commitment and her identification with Indian women and her acceptance by other Indian women in the movement.

69. Gabriele Dietrich, *One day i shall be like a banyan tree* (Belgium: Dileep S. Kamat, 1985).

70. Popular Korean drink.

71. Suh Nam Dong, *In Search of Minjung Theology* (Seoul, Korea: Kankil Sa, 1983), pp. 355-56. Translation and emphasis mine.

72. Anonymous, "From Jaini Bi—With Love," in O'Grady, p. 11. The editor explains that the Jaini Bi stands for all people who suffer extreme deprivation in a seemingly uncaring world but who receive a spark of hope from humanitarian concerns and actions.

5. Who Is Mary for Today's Asian Women?

1. Anonymous poem entitled "Mary Song," from "Mariology: A Pakena Perspective," Consultation on Asian Women's Theology—1987, pp. 2-3.

2. Ibid., p. 1.

3. Ibid.

4. Katoppo, *Compassionate and Free*, p. 21.

5. "Mariology: A Pakena Perspective," p. 1.

6. Katoppo, *Compassionate and Free*, p. 17.

7. Ibid., p. 73

8. Ibid.

9. "Mariology: A Pakena Perspective," pp. 1-2.

10. See the poem "Mary Song" at the beginning of this chapter.

11. "Mariology: A Pakena Perspective," p. 1.

12. Astrid Lobo, "Mary and the Woman of Today," *IGI* (September 1988), p. 7.

13. "Summary Statement on Mariology," Consultation on Asian Women's Theology—1987, p. 1.

14. See the poem "Mary Song" at the beginning of this chapter.

15. Katoppo, *Compassionate and Free*, p. 21.

16. Ibid., p. 20.

17. Ibid.

18. Ibid.

19. Ibid.

20. Ibid.

21. Han Kuk Yum, "Mariology as a Base for Feminist Liberation Theology," Consultation on Asian Women's Theology—1987, p. 3.

22. "Summary Statement on Mariology," p. 1.

23. Han Kuk Yum, p. 3.

24. Katoppo, *Compassionate and Free*, p. 21.

25. "Who Is Mary?" in *Proceedings: Asian Women's Consultation* (Manila: EATWOT, 1985), p. 156.

26. Lobo, "Mary and the Woman of Today," p. 7.

27. Ibid., pp. 7-8.

28. Nalaan, Navaratnarajah, "Mariology," Consultation on Asian Women's Theology—1987, p. 1.

29. "Summary Statement on Mariology," p. 1.

30. "Who Is Mary?" p. 156.

31. Ibid., p. 155.

32. Ibid. Emphasis mine.

33. Lobo, "Mary and the Women of Today," p. 11.

34. Anrora Zambrano, "Mariology," Consultation on Asian Women's Theology–1987, p. 6.

35. "Summary Statement on Mariology," p. 2.

36. Ibid., p. 2.

37. Ruth Ong, "A Woman of Faith and Hope," Consultation on Asian Women's Theology—1987, p. 3.

38. Han Kuk Yum, p. 2.

39. "Summary Statement on Mariology," p. 2.

40. Ibid., p. 2.

41. Virginia Fabella, "Mission of Women in the Church in Asia: Role and Position," *IGI* (December 1985), p. 82.

42. Ibid.

43. Lobo, "Mary and the Women of Today," p. 11.

44. "Who Is Mary?" p. 155.

45. Katoppo, *Compassionate and Free*, p. 23.

46. Han Kuk Yum, p. 4.

47. Ibid., p. 5.

48. Loretto-Eugenia Mapa, interview with the author, Women's Theological Center, Boston, February 8, 1989.

49. See Han Kuk Yum, p. 7.

50. Emily Mei Ling Cheng, "Mariology," Consultation on Asian Women's Theology–1987, p. 5.

51. Loretto-Eugenia Mapa, interview with the author, Women's Theology Center, Boston, February 8, 1989.

52. Ibid.

6. Emerging Asian Women's Spirituality

1. Ting Ling, untitled poem, in O'Grady, p. 46. Ting Ling is from China. At first, I hesitated to quote the poem due to its seemingly individualistic perspective. But I changed my mind later because of the concrete historical context of this poem, which was written in a China undergoing massive structural change.

2. Mary John Mananzan and Lee Sun Ai, "Emerging Spirituality of Asian Women," in Fabella and Oduyoye, p. 79.

3. "Women's Spirituality—Workshop Report," Consultation on Asian Women's Theology—1987, p. 1.

4. Ibid.

5. Ibid.

6. Mary John Mananzan, "Emerging Spirituality of Women: The Asian Experience," in *Essays on Women*, p. 149.

7. Stella Faria, "Feminist Spirituality: Emerging Trends," Consultation on Asian Women's Theology—1987, p. 1.

8. "Women's Spirituality—Workshop Report," p. 1.

9. Mananzan, *Essays on Women*, p. 150.

10. Ibid., pp. 149-50.

11. Ibid., p. 150.

12. Faria, pp. 3-4.

13. Mananzan, *Essays on Women*, p. 150.

14. Ibid., p. 151.

15. Mananzan and Lee, in Fabella and Oduyoye, p. 79.

16. Ibid., p. 79.

17. Ibid.

18. Mary Dunn, "Emerging Asian Women Spirituality," Consultation on Asian Women's Theology—1987, p. 1.

19. Ibid.

20. Ibid., p. 3.

21. Mananzan, *Essays on Women*, p. 152.

22. Ibid.

23. "Spirituality," Consultation on Asian Women's Theology—1987, p. 1.

24. Ibid.

25. Ibid., p. 2.

26. Mananzan and Lee, in Fabella and Oduyoye, p. 81.

27. Ibid.

28. Ibid., p. 82.

29. Ibid.

30. Mercy Mathew, "The Story of a Continuous Search," *IGI* (April 1985), p. 10.

31. Ibid.

32. Ibid., p. 7.

33. Ibid., p. 9.

34. Ibid., p. 11. Emphasis mine.

35. Mananzan, *Essays on Women*, p. 152.

36. Ibid., p. 151.

37. "Women's Spirituality—Workshop Report," pp. 1-2.

38. Mananzan and Lee, in Fabella and Oduyoye, p. 87.

39. Ibid., p. 84.

40. "Women's Spirituality-Workshop Report," p. 1.

41. Mananzan and Lee, in Fabella and Oduyoye, p. 80.

42. Ibid., pp. 79-80.

43. Ibid., p. 87.

44. This term should not be identified with the anti-abortionist slogan in the United States. When Asian women talk about pro-life spirituality, they mean literally pro-life for all living beings, not the Western context of opposing women's reproductive rights.

45. Mananzan and Lee, in Fabella and Oduyoye, p. 78.

46. Ibid.

47. Anita Nesiah, "Armed Conflict: Peace and Justice by Women?" This pamphlet was produced from her lecture for the Colloquium series at Bunting Institute, Radcliffe College, Cambridge, on March 1, 1988.

48. Ibid.

49. Ibid.

50. Ibid.

51. Mananzan and Lee, in Fabella and Oduyoye, p. 84.

52. Ibid.

53. Ibid.

54. Ibid., p. 85.

55. Ibid.

56. Loretto-Eugenia Mapa, interview with the author, Women's Theology Center, Boston, February 8, 1989.

57. *Ha-neu-Nim* is the name of a Korean indigenous God; it translates as Sky God. *Kwan-Woon-Chang-Nim* is a Warrior God in Korean shamanism. *Ye-Su-Nim* is the Korean name of Jesus.

58. Moon Dong Han, "Han—the Starting Point of New Life," in *The Story of Han*, ed. Suh Kwang Sun (Korea: The Borhee Press, 1988), p. 348. The translation is mine, with a few modifications.

59. Mananzan and Lee, in Fabella and Oduyoye, p. 87.

60. Ibid.

61. Mananzan, *Essays on Women*, p. 158.

62. Ibid.

63. According to the book *Pamathalaan: Ang Pagbubukas sa Tipanng Mahal na Ina* (*Spiritual Government: The Revelation of the Covenant with the Divine Mother*), the Philippines has a very important *Tipan* (covenant) with the Divine Mother.

64. Melane V. Talag, "The Power called Mother," *The Manila Chronicle* (February 22, 1988), p. 10.

65. Ibid.

66. Faria, p. 11.

67. Mananzan and Lee, in Fabella and Oduyoye, p. 84.

68. Ibid.

69. Faria, p. 9.

70. Mananzan and Lee, in Fabella and Oduyoye, p. 86.

71. Ibid.

72. Ibid.

73. Ibid.

74. Ibid.

75. Ibid.

76. Ibid., p. 87.

7. The Contribution and the Future

1. Kwok, "God Weeps With Our Own Pain," p. 90.

2. Tapia, p. 171.

3. Ibid.

4. See Gustavo Gutiérrez, *A Theology of Liberation* (Maryknoll, New York: Orbis Books, 1988).

5. See Kwok Pui-lan, "The Feminist Hermeneutics of Elisabeth Schüssler Fior-

enza: An Asian Feminist Response," *East Asia Journal of Theology* 3:2 (1985), pp. 147-53. See also idem., "Discovering the Bible in the Non-Biblical World," forthcoming in *Semeia*. See also Aruna Gnanadason, "Towards an Indian Feminist Theology I, II," two lectures presented at the Board of Theological Education's Institute of Teachers of Systematic Theologians, United Seminary in Bangalore, India, June 8-9, 1988.

EATWOT organized another Asian women's theological conference in Seoul, Korea, June 30-July 2, 1989, with two themes: "Patriarchy in Our Asian Reality" and "Asian Women's Hermeneutical Principle on the Basis of Our Reality." Under these themes, other questions were also asked: What does the oppression of women have to do with colonialism, economic exploitation, militarism, racism, and discrimination against minorities? In what way do all these forms of domination relate to the Bible and our Christian faith?

6. The terms "lived-world experience" and "the violence of abstraction" come from Beverly Harrison's presentation at the Women and Economics Seminar of the American Academy of Religion, November 1988.

7. The term *vision quest* is frequently used by Native Americans with specific cultural connotations. When I use the term, I simply mean Asian women's search for vision.

8. Lee Sung Hee, "Women's Liberation Theology as the Foundation for Asian Theology," *East Asia Journal of Theology* 4:2 (October 1986), pp. 12-13.

9. Tapia, preface.

10. To define the activity of creating theology as an echo was also suggested by the late minjung theologian Suh Nam Dong. Suh Nam Dong believes the exodus was the echo of Yahweh to the cries of the Hebrews under the tyranny of Egypt, and Amos' prophetic message to the corrupted society in northern Israel during 8 B.C. was his echo to the anger of Yahweh. Suh maintains that the rise of minjung theology in the last decade in Korea was the Korean theologian's echo of the cries of the minjung. He contends that the truthfulness of theology should be judged by the degree of authenticity and sensitivity of the echo the theologian makes to the cries of the poor. See Suh Nam Dong, *In Search of Minjung Theology*, preface.

11. Fabella, "Asian Women and Christology," p. 20.

12. Kim Yong Bok, "The Problem of Women and Socio-biography of Minjung," *The Task of Korean Women's Theology* (Seoul, Korea: KAWT, 1983), pp. 78-92.

13. Ibid.

14. We paid the equivalent of $5.00 U.S. each, a sum prostitutes in Manila commonly receive.

15. Kim Hee Eun, "Theological Reflection on Women's Work," *The Context of Korean Women's Theology* (Seoul, Korea: KAWT, 1985), p. 78.

16. Kwok, "Discovering the Bible in the Non-Biblical World."

17. Ibid., p. 17.

18. Ibid., p. 8. Korean minjung theologians established a landmark contribution to the conceptual "bringing together" of biblical and people's stories for theological reflection. See Suh Nam Dong, *In Search of Minjing Theology*; Kosuke Koyama, *Mount Fuji and Mount Sinai: A Critique of Idols* (Maryknoll, New York: Orbis Books, 1985); C. S. Song, *Tell Us Our Names: Story Theology from an Asian Perspective* (Maryknoll, New York: Orbis Books, 1984).

19. Kwok, "Discovering the Bible in the Non-Biblical World."

20. Chung Sook Ja, "General Comments," *IGI* (December 1984), pp. 22-23.

21. Some companies ask women to leave work when they get married or reach age twenty-five.

22. See KAWT, ed., *Women's Theology and Humanization* (Seoul, Korea: KAWT, 1987), pp. 70-91.

23. Ibid., p. 72.

24. Lee Oo Chung, "Our Hyun Jang and Women's Theology," in *Women's Theology and Humanization*, p. 89.

25. For more information on cosmic and meta-cosmic religion, see Aloysius Pieris, *An Asian Theology of Liberation* (Maryknoll, New York: Orbis Books, 1988), pp. 71-74. Note Pieris's *complementary* views on the relationship between cosmic religion and meta-cosmic religion. His complementary view is different from the prevailing view I describe here.

26. Note the different views on syncretism. See Hendrik Kraemer, *The Christian Message in a Non-Christian World* (Grand Rapids, Michigan: Kregel Publications, 1977); M. M. Thomas, *Risking Christ for Christ's Sake* (Geneva: WWC, 1987); Leonardo Boff, *Church, Charism, Power* (New York: Crossroads, 1985).

BIBLIOGRAPHY

Books

Abayasekera, J. and Niles, D. Preman, eds. *For the Dawning of the New*. Singapore: Christian Conference of Asia, 1981.

Anderson, Gerald H., ed. *Asian Voices in Christian Theology*. Maryknoll, New York: Orbis Books, 1976.

———. *Christ and Crisis in Southeast Asia*. New York: Friendship Press, 1968.

Anderson, Gerald H. and Stransky, Thomas F., eds. *Christ's Lordship & Religious Pluralism*. Maryknoll, New York: Orbis Books, 1981.

Arai, Tosh, ed. *Children of Asia*. Singapore: Christian Conference of Asia, 1979.

Ariarajah, S. Wesley. *The Bible and People of Other Faiths*. Maryknoll, New York: Orbis Books, 1989.

Asian Women's Consultation. *Proceedings: Asian Women's Consultation*. Manila: Ecumenical Association of Third World Theologians, 1985.

Association of Women in Theology. *Power from Powerlessness*. Philippines: AWIT, 1983.

Avia, C. R., reporter. *Peasant Theology: Reflection by the Filipino Peasants on Their Process of Social Revolution*. Book No. 1. Asia: World Student Christian Federation (WSCF), 1976

Balasuriya, Tissa. *The Eucharist and Human Liberation*. Maryknoll, New York: Orbis Books, 1979.

———. *Jesus Christ and Human Liberation*. Quest Series 48 (September 1976). Colombo, Sri Lanka: Centre for Society and Religion, 1976.

Berstein, Gail Lee. *Haruko's World: A Japanese Farm Woman and Her Community*. Stanford: Stanford University, 1980.

Bhasin, Kamla and Khan, Nighat Said. *Some Questions on Feminism and Its Relevance in South Asia*. Delhi: Kali for Women, 1986.

Brock, Rita N. *Journeys by Heart: A Christology of Erotic Power*. New York: Crossroad Publishing Company, 1988.

Centre for Society and Religion, ed. *A Hymn to Creation: Essays in Women and Religion*. Colombo, Sri Lanka: The Centre for Society and Religion, 1983.

———. *God, Women, and the Bible*. Columbo, Sri Lanka: The Centre for Society and Religion, 1983.

Christian Conference of Asia. *A Call to Vulnerable Discipleship*. Niles Memorial Lectures, Bible Studies and Testimonies of the Seventh Assembly, 1981.

———. *Liberation, Justice, Development*. Asian Ecumenical Conference for Development, July 14-22, 1970.

———. *Living in Christ in People*. The Seventh Assembly of the CCA, April 18 to May 28, 1981.

131

——. *Tradition and Innovation: A Search for Relevant Ecclesiology in Asia.* 1983.

——, ed. *Reading the Bible as Asian Women.* Singapore: CCA, 1986.

——, ed. *Women to Women: Asian Women in Solidarity: Mobilizing Women in Struggles for Food, Justice and Freedom.* Singapore: CCA, 1986.

Christian Conference of Asia—International Affairs. *Escape from Domination: A Consultation Report on Patterns of Domination and People's Movement in Asia.* 1980.

——. *People Against Domination: A Consultation Report on People's Movements and Structures of Domination in Asia.* Kuala Lumpur, Malaysia, February 24-28, 1981.

Christian Conference of Asia—Urban Rural Mission (URM). *Captives on the Land.* Report of a Consultation on Land. Colombo, February 1976.

——. *Christian Response to Race and Minority Issues in Asia.* Proceedings and Findings of a Regional Consultation organized by the CCA in cooperation with the WCC, March 24-29, 1980, New Delhi.

——. *From the Womb of Han, Stories of Korean Women Workers.* Hong Kong: 1982.

——. *Identity and Justice.* Report of an ad hoc meeting on Race and Minority Issues in Asia, Hong Kong, March 1977.

——. *In Clenched Fists of Struggle.* Report of the Workshop on the Impact of TNCs in Asia, 1981.

——. *No Place in the Inn: Voices of Minority People in Asia.* Hong Kong, 1979.

——. *Spirituality for Combat.* Hong Kong, 1983.

——. *Struggling with People is Living in Christ.* Hong Kong, 1981.

——. *Theology and Ideology: An Urban Rural Mission Discussion.* Hong Kong, 1980.

——. *A Study of Poor Women in Korea.* Seoul, Korea: Minjungsa, 1983.

Clarke, Jennie, ed. *Weaving New Patterns: Women's Struggle for Change in Asia and the Pacific.* Hong Kong: World Student Christian Federation Asia/Pacific Region, 1986.

Cochran, Jo, ed. *Gathering Ground: New Writing by Northwest Women of Color.* Seattle: Seal Press Feminist, 1984.

Commission on Theological Concerns—Christian Conference of Asia, ed. *Minjung Theology: People as the Subjects of History.* London: Zed Press, 1983; Maryknoll, New York: Orbis Books, 1983.

——, ed. *Towards the Sovereignty of the People: A Search for an Alternative Form of Democratic Politics in Asia—A Christian Discussion.* Singapore: Christian Conference of Asia, 1983.

Condon, Jane. *A Half Step Behind: Japanese Women of the 1980's.* New York: Dodd, Mead, 1985.

Cone, James H. *For My People.* Maryknoll, New York: Orbis Books, 1984.

——. *God of the Oppressed.* New York: Harper, 1975.

Croll, Elizabeth, *Feminism and Socialism in China.* London: Routledge & Kegan Paul, 1978.

Davies, Miranda, ed. *Third World-Second Sex*, Vol. 2. London and New Jersey: Zed Books Ltd., 1987.

Dawood, Nawaz. *Tea and Poverty: Plantations and the Political Economy of Sri Lanka.* Singapore: CCA-URM, 1980.

Delavignette, Robert. *Christianity and Colonialism.* Translated from the French by J. R. Foster. New York: Howthorn, 1964.

Dietrich, Gabriele. *One day i shall be like a banyan tree.* Belgium: Dileep S. Kamat, 1985.

Easton, Steward C. *The Rise and Fall of Western Colonialism*. New York and London: Fredrick A. Praeger, 1964.

Elwood, Douglas J., ed. *Asian Christian Theology: Emerging Themes*. Philadelphia: The Westminster Press, 1980.

——. *What Asian Christians are Thinking*. Philippines: New Day Publishers, 1976.

Elwood, Douglas J. and Nacpil, Emerito P., eds. *The Human and the Holy: Asian Perspectives in Christian Theology*. Philippines: New Day Publishers, 1978.

England, John. *Theology in Action 2: A Workshop Report for Malaysia and Singapore, March 1-12, 1973*. Kuala Lumpur: East Asia Christian Conference.

——, ed. *Living Theology in Asia*. Maryknoll, New York: Orbis Books, 1982.

England, John and Oh Jae shik, eds. *Theology in Action: A Workshop Report*. September 1-12, 1972.

Fabella, Virgina, ed. *Asia's Struggle for Full Humanity*. Maryknoll, New York: Orbis Books, 1980.

Fabella, Virginia and Lee Sun Ai, eds. *We Dare To Dream: Doing Theology as Asian Women*. Seoul: Asian Women's Resource Center, 1989; Maryknoll, New York: Orbis Books, 1990.

Fabella, Virginia and Oduyoye, Mercy A., eds. *With Passion and Compassion: Third World Women Doing Theology*. Maryknoll, New York: Orbis Books, 1988.

Fabella, Virginia and Torres, Sergio, eds. *Doing Theology in a Divided World*. Maryknoll, New York: Orbis Books, 1985.

——. *Irruption of the Third World: Challenge to Theology*. Maryknoll, New York: Orbis Books, 1983.

Federation of Asian Bishops' Conference. *The Role of Women in the Church as a Community of Faith in Asia*. Thailand, October 1982.

Floro, Sergy and Luz, Nana, eds. *Sourcebook on Philippine Women in Struggle*. Berkeley: Philippine Resource Center, 1985.

Gabriela. *Gabriela: Assembly Proceedings*. Philippines, 1984.

Gheddo, Piero. *Why Is the Third World Poor?* Maryknoll, New York: Orbis Books, 1973.

Gnanadason, Aruna, ed. *Towards a Theology of Humanhood: Women's Perspectives*. Delhi: All India Council of Christian Women, 1986.

Guisso, Richard, ed. *Women in China: Current Directions in Historical Scholarship*. New York: Philo, 1981.

Gutiérrez, Gustavo. *A Theology of Liberation*. Translated and edited by Sister Caridad Inda and John Eagleson. Maryknoll, New York: Orbis Books, 1973.

Hao Yap Kim, ed. *Asian Theological Reflections on Suffering and Hope*. Asia Focus. Singapore: CCA, 1977.

Harrington, Michael. *The Vast Majority: A Journey to the World's Poor*. New York: Simon and Schuster, 1977.

Harrison, Beverly W. *Making the Connections*. Boston: Beacon Press, 1985.

Heyward, Isabel Carter. *The Redemption of God: A Theology of Mutual Relations*. Washington, D.C.: University Press of America, Inc., 1982.

Hick, John. *God and the Universe of Faiths: Essays in the Philosophy of Religion*. London: The Macmillan Press Ltd., 1973.

Holden, Peter et al. *Tourism, Prostitution and Development*. Ecumenical Coalition on Third World Tourism, 1983.

Hong, Evelyn. *Malaysian Women: Problems and Issues*. Penang: Consumer Association of Penang (CAP), 1983.

——. *See the Third World While It Lasts*. Penang: CAP, 1985.

IDOC Dossier No. 7. *The Future of the Missionary Enterprise: Mission Through People's Organization*. South Korea, Rome: 1974.

International Affairs—WCC. *Human Rights in the Republic of Korea*. Geneva: WCC, 1979.

Ishimoto, Shidzue. *Facing Two Ways: The Story of My Life*. Stanford: Stanford University, 1984.

Japanese Catholic Council for Justice and Peace, ed. *"A Declaration of Conscience:" The Korean Catholic Church and Human Rights*. 3 Vols. Maryknoll, New York: Orbis Books, 1983.

Jayawardena, Kumari. *Feminism and Nationalism in the Third World*, London: Zed Books Ltd, 1986.

——. *Feminism in Sri Lanka in the Decade, 1975-1985*. Colombo, Sri Lanka: Women's Education Centre, 1986.

——. *Liberalism and the Women's Movement*. Columbo, Sri Lanka: Centre for Society and Religion (Education Unit) and Women's Education Centre, 1985.

Johnson, Kay Ann. *Women, The Family and Peasant in China*. Chicago: University of Chicago, 1983.

Katoppo, Marianne. *Compassionate and Free: An Asian Woman's Theology*. Maryknoll, New York: Orbis Books, 1980.

Kendall, Laruel. *Shamans, Housewives, and Other Restless Spirits: Women in Korean Ritual Life*. Honolulu: University of Hawaii Press, 1985.

Kikumura, Akemi. *Through Harsh Winters: The Life of a Japanese Immigrant Woman*. Novato, CA: Chandler & Sharp Publisher, 1981.

——. *The Gold-Crowned Jesus and Other Writings*. Edited by Kim Chong Sun and Shelly Killen. Maryknoll, New York: Orbis Books, 1978.

Kingston, Maxine Hong. *The Woman Warrior*. New York: Alfred A. Knopf, 1976.

Kitamori, Kazoh. *Theology of the Pain of God*. Richmond, Virginia: John Knox Press, 1958.

Korea Church Women United. *Kisaeng Tourism: A Nation-Wide Survey Report on Conditions in Four Areas: Seoul, Pusan, Cheju, Kwangju*. Seoul, Korea: Church Women United, 1984.

Korea Theological Study Institute, ed. *Essays on Minjung*. Seoul, Korea: Korea Theological Study Institute, 1984.

Korean Association of Women Theologians. *The Context of Korean Women's Theology*. Seoul, Korea: KAWT, 1985.

——. *Second Consultation for the Establishment of Feminist Theology in Asia*. Seoul, Korea: KAWT, October 1984.

——. *The Task of Korean Women's Theology*. Seoul, Korea: KAWT, 1985.

——, ed. *Women's Theology and Humanization*. Seoul, Korea: KAWT, 1987.

Koyama, Kosuke. *Mount Fuji and Mount Sinai: A Critique of Idols*. Maryknoll, New York: Orbis Books, 1985.

Lebra, Takie S. *Japanese Women: Constraint and Fulfillment*. Honolulu: University of Hawaii, 1984.

Lee Sun Ai, and Luce, Don, eds. *The Wish: Poems of Contemporary Korea*. New York: Friendship Press, 1983.

Liddle, Joanna and Joshi, Rama. *Daughters of Independence: Gender, Caste and Class in India*. London: Zed Books Ltd., 1986.

Loh I To, ed. *New Song of Asian Cities*. Singapore: CCA-URM, 1972.

Lorde, Audrey. *Sister Outsider*. New York: The Crossing Press, 1984.

Mananzan, Mary J., ed. *Essays on Women*. Manila: Woman's Studies Program, Saint Scholastica's College, 1987.

——, ed. *Woman and Religion*. Manila: The Institute of Women's Studies, Saint Scholastica's College, 1988.

——, ed. *Women in Asia: Status and Image*. Asia Focus. Singapore: CCA, 1979.

Matsubara, Hisako. *Cranes at Dusk*. Dial Press, 1985.

McCoy, Charles S. *When Gods Change*. Nashville: Abingdon Press, 1980.

McFague, Sallie. *Metaphorical Theology*. Philadelphia: Fortress Press, 1982.

Miles, Maria. *Patriarchy and Accumulation on a World Scale: Women in the International Division of Labour*. London: Zed Books Ltd., 1986.

——. *The Social Origins of the Sexual Division of Labour*. Colombo, Sri Lanka: Women's Education Centre, 1985.

——. *Utopian Socialism and Women's Emancipation*. Colombo, Sri Lanka: Centre for Society and Religion (Education Unit) and Women's Education Centre, 1985.

Moon, Cyrus. *A Korean Minjung Theology: An Old Testament Perspective*. Maryknoll, New York: Orbis Books, 1985.

Moraga, Cherrie and Anzaldua, Gloria, ed. *This Bridge Called Me Back*. New York: Kitchen Table: Women of Color Press, 1981.

Nacpil, Emerito P. and Elwood, Douglas J., eds. *The Human and the Holy: Asian Perspectives in Christian Theology*. Maryknoll, New York: Orbis Books, 1980.

National Conference of Asian Women Theologians (Northeast U.S. Group). *An Ocean with Many Shores: Asian Women Making Connections in Theology and Ministry*. New York: Asian Women Theologians, 1986.

Neill, Stephen. *Colonialism and Christian Missions*. New York: McGraw Hill, 1966.

Nelson, Marlin L. *The How and Why of Third World Missions: An Asian Case Study*. Pasadena, California: William Carey Library, 1976.

——, ed. *Reading in Third World Missions: A Collection of Essential Documents*. Pasadena, California: William Carey Library, 1976.

Niebuhr, H. Richard. *Christ and Culture*. New York and London: Harper & Row, 1975.

Niles, Preman and Thomas, T. K., eds. *Witnessing to the Kingdom*. Asia Focus. Singapore: CCA, 1979.

Noh, Jong Sun. *Religion and Just Revolution: The Third World Perspective*. Hamden, Connecticut: Center for Asian Theology, 1984.

North American Coalition for Human Rights in Korea. *Documents on Human Rights Struggle in Korea 1978*. New York, 1978.

Ogle, George E. *Liberty to the Captives: The Struggle Against Oppression in South Korea*. Atlanta: John Knox Press, 1978.

O'Grady, Alison, ed. *Inheritors of the Earth* (Report of the People's Forum on People, Land, and Justice). Singapore: CCA-URM, 1981.

——, ed. *Voices of Women: An Asian Anthology*. Singapore: Asian Christian Women's Conference, 1978.

O'Grady, Ron. *Tourism in the Third World*. Maryknoll, New York: Orbis Books, 1982.

Ohara, Miyao, trans. and ed. *The Songs of Hiroshima: Anthology*. Hiroshima: Shunyo-sha Shuppan Co. Ltd., 1979.

Panikkar, Raimundo. *The Intra-Religious Dialogue*. New York and New Jersey: Paulist Press, 1978.

Park Soon Kyung. *Korean Nation and the Task of Women's Theology*. Seoul, Korea: Hyundae Shinsuh, 1983.

———. *Unification of the Nation and Christianity*. Seoul, Korea: Daehan Keedokyo Suhwhe, 1983.

Paul, Diana Y. *Women in Buddhism, Images of the Feminine in the Mahayana Tradition*. Berkeley: University of California Press, 1985.

Phongpaichit, Pasuk. *From Peasant Girls to Bangkok Masseuses*. Geneva: ILO, 1982.

Pieris, Aloysius. *An Asian Theology of Liberation*. Maryknoll, New York: Orbis Books, 1988.

Pobee, John S. and Von Wartenberg-Potter, Bärbel, eds. *New Eyes for Reading: Biblical and Theological Reflections by Women from the Third World*. Oak Park, Illinois: Meyer Stone Books, 1986.

Robins-Mowey, Dorothy. *The Hidden Sun: Women of Modern Japan*. Boulder, CO: Westview, 1983

Romero, Flerida Ruth. *Women and the Law*. University of the Philippines Law Center and the Asia Foundation, 1983.

Ruether, Rosemary R. *Sexism and God-Talk*. Boston: Beacon Press, 1983.

Russell, Letty, M., ed. *Changing Contexts of Our Faith*. Philadelphia: Fortress Press, 1985.

Russell, Letty M., Kwok, Pui-lan, Isasi-Diaz, Ada M., and Cannon, Katie G., eds. *Inheriting Our Mother's Gardens: Feminist Theology in Third World Perspective*. Philadelphia: The Westminster Press, 1988.

Said, Edward W. *Orientalism*. New York: Vintage Books, 1978.

Samartha, Stanley J. *Courage for Dialogue: Ecumenical Issues in Inter-Religious Relationships*. Geneva: WCC, 1981.

Schreiter, Robert J. *Constructing Local Theologies*. Maryknoll, New York: Orbis Books, 1986

Schüssler Fiorenza, Elisabeth. *In Memory of Her*. New York: Crossroad, 1984.

——— and Carr, Anne, eds. *Women, Work, and Poverty*. Edinburgh: T&T Clark Ltd., 1987.

Segundo, Juan Luis. *The Liberation of Theology*. Maryknoll, New York: Orbis Books, 1976.

Song, Cathy. *Picture Bride*. New Haven: Yale University, 1983.

Song, C.S. *The Compassionate God*. Maryknoll, New York: Orbis Books, 1982.

———. *The Tears Of Lady Meng: A Parable of People's Political Theology*. Maryknoll, New York: Orbis Books, 1982.

———. *Theology from the Womb of Asia*. Maryknoll, New York: Orbis Books, 1986.

Sugimoto, Etsu I. *Daughter of the Samurai*. Arden Library, 1977.

Suh, David Kwang-sun. *Religion and the Revolt of the Oppressed*. Delhi: ISPCK, 1981.

———. *Theology, Ideology, and Culture*. Colombo, Sri Lanka: Centre for Society and Religion, 1985.

Thomas, M. M. *Risking Christ for Christ's Sake*. Geneva: WCC, 1987.

Tillich, Paul. *Christianity and the Encounter of World Religions*. New York: Columbia University Press, 1964.

Torres, Sergio and Eagleson, John, eds. *The Challenge of Basic Christian Communities*. Maryknoll, New York: Orbis Books, 1981.

Torres, Sergio and Fabella, Virginia, eds. *The Emergent Gospel*. Maryknoll, New York: Orbis Books, 1978.

———, eds. *Irruption of the Third World: Challenge to Theology*. Maryknoll, New York: Orbis Books, 1984.

Verhese, Jamila. *Her Gold and Her Body*. Hyderabad: Vikas Publishing House, 1980.

———. *No Other Name: The Choice Between Syncretism and Christian Universalism*. Philadephia: Westminster Press, 1963.

Visser't Hooft, Willem. *Has the Ecumenical Movement a Future?* Belfast: Christian Journal Limited, 1974.

Webster, John C. B. and Webster, Ellen Low, eds. *The Church and Women in the Third World*. Philadelphia: The Westminster Press, 1985.

Wolf, M. and Ritke, R., eds. *Women in Chinese Society*. Stanford: Stanford University, 1976.

Woodsmall, Ruth F., ed. *Eastern Women: Today and Tomorrow*. Boston: The General Committee on the United Study of Foreign Missions, 1933.

Wynne, Alison. *No Time for Crying*. Hong Kong: Resource Centre for Philippine Concern, 1979.

Zinkin, Taya. *Caste in India: Yesterday and Today*. New York: Bantam Books, 1970.

Articles

Abeyesekera, Sunila, Bastian, Sunil and Siriwardena, Reggie. "Patriarchy and Capitalism." *Logos*, November 1982.

Ahlstrand, Kajsa. "A Woman's Universe." *Logos*, May 1986.

Ahn Sang Nim. "My Understanding of Feminist Theology." *In God's Image*, April 1985.

Alexander, Anna V. "Female Genital Mutilation." *In God's Image*, June-September 1986.

Alexander, Philip. "Child Birth: A Medical Student's Reflection." *In God's Image*, June-September 1986.

Ariola, Fe. "Women's Place in the Struggle." *Kalinangan*, October 1985.

Asedillo, Rebecca. "A New Picture of Mary: A View from Below." *In God's Image*, April 1985.

———. "Singing their Song in a Troubled Land." *Voices from the Third World*, December 1982.

Balai. "Airline Ads: Selling An Image." *Balai*, Vol. 2. No. 4.

———. "The Buying Power of Female Labor." *Balai*, Vol. 2, No. 4.

———. "Cheap Asian Female Labor and the Run-Away Shops." *Balai*, Vol. 2, No.4.

———. "Comparative Study of Women Workers in Asia." *Balai*, Vol. 2, No. 4.

———. "The Cultural Roots of Asian Female Subjugation." *Balai*, Vol. 2, No. 4.

———. "The Geopolitics of Prostitution." *Balai*, Vol. 2, No. 4.

———. "Historical Tid-bits of Prostitution in Japan." *Balai*, Vol. 2, No. 4.

———. "The Marriage Market." *Balai*, Vol. 2, No. 4.

———. "The Oriental Christ: A Feminist." *Balai*, Vol. 2, No. 4.

———. "Rural Poverty and Other Issues." *Balai*, Vol. 2, No. 4.

———. "Springboard for Liberation Valiant Women." *Balai*, Vol. 2, No. 4

———. "The Third World Movement Against Exploitation." *Balai*, Vol. 2, No. 4.

———. "Working Women from 1965-2000." *Balai*, Vol. 2, No. 4.

———. "The Yin and Yang of Asian Women." *Balai*, Vol. 2, No. 4, December 1981.

Balasuriya, Tissa."Mary a Mature Committed Woman." *Logos*, August 1984.

------. "New Forms of Exploitation." *Logos*, December 1981.

------. "Women and Men in the New Community." *Logos*, November 1982.

Brunerova, Bozena. "Women in Socialist Society." *Logos*, November 1982.

Carter, Aiko. "Women in Church and Society—A Japanese Perspective." *In God's Image*, December 1985.

Chang Sang. "Mission and Competence of Church Women in Korea." *In God's Image*, December 1985.

Chawla, Janet. "Women Power Is Also Birthing Power." *In God's Image*, December 1986.

Chinniah, Malar. "Women in the Early Church and the Interpretation of Pauline Text in Relation to Women Today." *In God's Image*, October 1985.

Christian Conference of Asia. "Backstreet Guide to Degrading Slavery." *CCA News*, Vol. 23, No. 1/2, January/February 1988.

Christiane, "Pathetic Women of the Slums." *Logos*, December 1981.

Chung Hyun Kyung. "Following Naked Dancing and Long Dreaming." *Inheriting Our Mother's Gardens: Feminist Theology in Third World Perspective*, Letty Russell, Kwok Pui Lan, Ada Maria Isasi-Diaz, Katie Cannon, eds., Philadelphia: The Westminster Press, 1988.

------. "Han-pu-ri: Doing Theology from Korean Women's Perspective." *The Ecumenical Review*, Vol. 40, No. 1, January 1987. Reprinted in Virginia Fabella and Lee Sun Ai, eds., *We Dare To Dream*, Maryknoll, New York: Orbis Books, 1990.

------. "Opium or the Seed of Revolution?: Shamanism, Women Centered Religiosity in Korea." *Concilium*, May 1988.

Cone, James H. "Ecumenical Association of Third World Theologians." *Ecumenical Trends*, Vol. 14, No. 8, September 1985.

Consultation on Asian Women's Theology, Singapore, November 20-28, 1989. "Summary Statement on Mariology." Forthcoming by *In God's Image*.

------. Anonymous. "Mariology: A Pakena Perspective." Unpublished paper.

------. Anonymous. "Spirituality." Unpublished paper.

------. Arayapraatep, Komol. "Christology." Unpublished paper.

------. Cheng, Emily Mei Ling. "Mariology." Unpublished paper.

------. Choi, Man Ja. "Feminist Christology." Unpublished paper.

------. Dunn, Mary. "Emerging Asian Women's Spirituality." Unpublished paper.

------. Han Kuk Yum. "Mariology as a base for Feminist Liberation Theology." Unpublished paper.

------. Melanchton, Monica. "Christology and Women." Unpublished paper.

------. Nalaan, Navaratnarajah. "Mariology." Unpublished paper.

------. Ong, Ruth. "A Woman of Faith and Hope." Unpublished paper.

------. Zambrano, Anrora. "Mariology." Unpublished paper.

Consultation Report from Theologically Trained Women of the Philippines. "A Continuing Challenge for Women's Ministry." *In God's Image*, August 1983.

Derego, Pearl et al. "The Exodus Story." *In God's Image*, September 1988.

de Silva, Narada. "Sri Lankan Housemaid in the Middle East." *Logos*, December 1981.

Dietrich, Gabriele. "The Origin of the Bible Revisited: Reconstructing Women's History." *Logos*, May 1986.

------. "Perspective of a Feminist Theology: Toward a Full Humanity of Women and Men." Unpublished Paper, India, 1986.

------. "Perspective of a Feminist Theology." *Logos*, October 1983.

——. "Recapturing Women's Creativity." *In God's Image*, December 1984.

D'Sousa, Lucy. "My Sadhana." *In God's Image*, September 1988.

Esquivelo, Julia. "Liberation Theology and Women." *Logos*, October 1983.

Eugenia, Mary. "Women in Islamic Faith." *In God's Image*, December 1986.

Fabella, Virginia. "Asian Women and Christology." *In God's Image*, September 1987.

——. "Mission of Women in the Church in Asia: Role and Position." *In God's Image*, December 1985.

Fernando, Milburga. "Towards a Theology of Womanhood." *Logos*, May 1986.

Fernando, Nimalka. "The Meaning of Mariology for Us Today." *Kalinangan*, June 1985.

——. "Towards a Theology Related to a Full Humanity." *In God's Image*, April 1985.

Gallup, Padma. "Doing Theology—An Asian Feminist Perspective." *CTC Bulletin*, December 1983.

——. "The New Community of Asia." *Ecumenical Review*, 34:2, 1982.

Geaga, Gloria Maiv. "Violence in Women's Lives: A Global Perspective." *Kalinangan*, June 1985.

Gnanadason, Aruna. "Human Rights and Women's Concerns." *Religion and Society*, 28:1.

——. "The Search For Humanhood—A New Hermeneutical Approach." *Atesea Occasional Papers*, June 1987.

Goonatileka, Hema. "The Position of Women in Buddhism." *Logos*, November 1982.

Hensman, Pauline. "Mary Speaks." *In God's Image*, October 1985.

——. "The Risen Christ and Ending the Oppression and Subjugation of Women, the Poor and the Downtrodden." *Logos*, May 1986.

Hirota, Filo. "The Church in Japan is a Women's Church?" *In God's Image*, December 1986.

Honclada, Jurgette. "Notes on Women & Christ in Philippines." *In God's Image*, October 1985.

IDOC Documentation Service. "Korean Women in Ministry." *IDOC Bulletin*, No. 8-9, 1984.

Indian National Council of Churches. "Church Women Struggling: Two Cases in Point." *Kalinangan*, June 1983.

Ismail, Jezima. "A Statement on the Status, Role, and Responsibility of the Muslim Woman." *Logos*, May 1986.

Jayawardena, Kumari. "Feminism and Nationalism in the Third World." *Logos*, November 1982.

Joseph, Susan. "I am a Woman." *In God's Image*, September 1988.

Katoppo, Marianne. "Mother Jesus." *Logos*, October 1983.

——. "Perspective for a Woman's Theology." *Voices of the Third World*, September 1985.

——. "Women's Liberation from an Indonesian (Mihanassan) Perspective." *Logos*, November 1982.

Kim Ai Young. "Theological Reflections on the Agriculture Situation." *In God's Image*, April 1985.

Kim Hee Eun. "Theological Reflection on Women's Work." *The Context of Korean Women's Theology*, Seoul: KAWT, 1985.

Kim Young Hee. "Theological Reflection on the Situation of the Urban Poor." *In God's Image*, April 1985.

Korean Association of Women Theologians, "Consultation Toward the Establishing of Asian Feminist Theology." *CTC Bulletin*, December 1983.

Korean Feminist Collective. "A Discussion on Feminism." *Asian Women*, Vol. 11, No. 36, September 1986.

Kuninobu, Junko Wada. "Women's Studies in Japan." *Women's Studies International Forum*, 7:4 (1984).

Kwok, Pui-lan. "Discovering the Bible in the Non-Biblical World." Forthcoming in *Semeia*.

———. "The Emergence of Asian Feminist Consciousness on Culture and Theology." Unpublished paper.

———. "The Feminist Hermeneutics of Elizabeth Schüssler Fiorenza: An Asian Feminist Response." *East Asia Journal of Theology*, Vol. 3, No. 2., 1985.

———. "God Weeps with Our Pain." *CTC Bulletin*, December 1983.

Lascano, Lydia. "The Role of Women in the Church and Society." *In God's Image*, December 1985-February 1986.

Lateef, Shahida. "Attitudes Towards Women in Islam." *Logos*, November 1982.

Lee Chong Ai. "Awake, Rise and Sing." *In God's Image*, December 1985 – February 1986.

Lee Oo Chung. "Korean Culture and Feminist Theology." *In God's Image*, September 1987.

Lee Sun Ai. "Asian Women's Theological Reflection." *East Asia Journal of Theology*, 3:2, 1985.

———. "Image of God." *In God's Image*, September 1988.

———. "A Reading from a Taoist Funeral Song Designed for Women." *In God's Image*, April 1984.

———. "The Women's Movement and Ecumenical Agenda." Seoul, Korea: Hyundae Shinsuh, 1983.

Lee Sun Ai and Yayori, Matsui. "Theological Reflections on the Prostitution Industry." *Women in Third World Theology*, September 1985.

Lee Sung Hee. "Women's Liberation Theology as the Foundation for Asian Theology." *East Asia Journal of Theology*, Vol. 4, No. 2, October 1986.

Lewis, Nantawan Boonprasat. "Asian Women Theology: A Historical and Theological Analysis." *East Asian Journal of Theology* IV, October 1986.

———. "Human Rights for Asian Women: Toward a Fuller Actualization." *Human Rights and the Global Mission of the Church*, Boston Theological Institute Annual Series, I, 1985.

———. "An Overview of the Role of Women in Asia – A Perspective and Challenge to Higher Education." *East Asia Journal of Theology*, October 1985.

Ligo, Arche. "Liberation Themes in Phillippine Religiosity." *Pintig Diwa Faculty Journal VIII*, 1988.

Lobo, Astrid. "Mary and the Women of Today." *In God's Image*, September 1988.

———. "My Image of God." *In God's Image*, September 1988.

Mananzan, Mary John. "Prophecy as Resistance – A Philippine Experience." *Voices of the Third World*, September 1985.

———. "Theology from the Point of View of Asian Women." Paper presented to Asian women EATWOT members, Manila, 1986.

Mascarenhas, Marie Mignon. "Female Infanticide and Foeticide in India." *Stree* (an occasional newsletter of the All India Council of Christian Women), No. 16, October 1987.

Mathew, Mercy. "The Story of a Continuous Search." *In God's Image*, April 1985.

Monterio, Rita. "My Image of God." *In God's Image*, September 1988.

New Zealand Women's Conference. "Women's Space — Spirituality — Ministry." *In God's Image*, December 1984.

Niles, D. Preman. "Some Emerging Theological Trends in Asia." *CTC Bulletin*, March 1981.

Niquidula, Lydia N. "Women in Theology Revolutionizing Liturgy." *CTC Bulletin*, December 1983.

Park Soon Kyung. "Summing Up the Total Program of the Korean Women's Theological Consultation." *In God's Image*, April 1985.

Parkin, Harry. "Confucian Thoughts on Women." *CTC Bulletin*, December 1983.

Perera, Angela. "Women in the Plantation Sector." *Logos*, December 1981.

Rebera, Audrey. "Woman and Man in the Bible." *Logos*, October 1983.

Rivera, Dazzel K. "Asian Women Down Under." *Balai*, No. 12, June 1981.

Salgado, Nirmala. "Images of the Feminine in Religion with Special Reference to Christian, Buddhist, and Hindu Scriptures." *Logos*, May 1986.

Selvi, Y. and Manorama, Ruth. "Theological Reflections on our Experience in the Struggle of Women in the Oppressed Section of Society." *Voices of the Third World*, September 1985.

Sigrid. "Through Women's Eyes." *In God's Image*, December, 1985/ February 1986.

Silva, Bernadeen. "Biblical Message of Equality." *Logos*, October 1983.

——. "Capitalism and Women." *Logos*, November 1982.

——. "Spirituality of Sexuality." *The Voices of the Third World*, September 1985.

——. "What then is Feminist Theology?" *Logos*, May 1986.

Skuse, Jean. "The Ecumenical Movement from a Feminist Perspective." *CTC Bulletin*, December 1983.

Stephens, Alexandra. "Migration & Women Heads of Rural Households." *Balai*, No. 12, June 1981.

Swaris, J.N. "Women in the Old Testament." *Logos*, October 1983.

Talag, Melane V. "The Power Called Mother." *The Manila Chronicle*, February 22, 1988.

Thiruchandran, Selvi. "Women in Hinduism." *Logos*, November 1982.

Thitsa, Khin. "The Conditions of Female Consciousness in Chiengmai Province, Thailand." *Logos*, November 1982.

——. "Providence and Prostitution: Image and Reality for Women in Buddhist Thailand." Unpublished paper.

Thomas, M. M. "Some Notes on a Christian Interpretation of Nationalism in Asia." *South East Asian Journal of Theology*, 1960.

Wall, Lynne. "Power is a Dirty Word." *In God's Image*, December 1984.

Women Participants in CCA Ecclesiology Meeting. "Realities of the Asian Women in Society and Church." *In God's Image*, December 1986.

Women's Groups Workshop. "Militarisation and Militarism: A Women's Perspective Part II-On Militarisation and the National Security State." *Quest*, November 1986.

——. "Women Against Racism and Militarisation Part I-Nationalism and Racism." *Quest*, September 1986.

Yayori, Matsui. "Asian Population Policies and How They Oppress Women." *In God's Image*, December 1986.

Dissertations and Theses
Chung Sook Ja. "An Attempt At Feminist Theology In Korea." M. Div. thesis, San Francisco Theological Seminary, 1986.

Kwok Pui-lan. "Chinese Women and Christianity 1860-1929." Ph.D. dissertation, Harvard Divinity School, 1988.

Lee Ock Kyung. "A Study on Formational Condition and Settlement Mechanism of Jeong Juel Ideology of Yi Dynasty." M.A. thesis, Ewha Women's University, 1985.

Suh Chang Won. "A Formulation of Minjung Theology: Toward a Socio-Historical Theology of Asia." Ph. D. dissertation, Union Theological Seminary, 1986.

Tapia, Elizabeth. "The Contribution of Philippine Christian Women to Asian Women's Theology." Ph.D. dissertation, Claremont Graduate School, 1989.

Lectures and Interviews
Cho Wha Soon. Interview in New York, May 1986.

Gnanadason, Aruna. "Towards an Indian Feminist Theology I, II." Two lectures at the Board of Theological Education's Institute of Teachers of Systematic Theologians at United Seminary, Bangalore, India, June 8-9, 1988.

Hyun Young Hak. "Minjung the Suffering Servant and Hope." Lecture given at Union Theological Seminary, New York, April 1982.

———. "Theology with Sweat, Tears and Laughter." Lecture given at Union Theological Seminary, New York, November 1982.

Lee Sun Ai. Interview at Interchurch Center, New York, August 9, 1988.

Mapa, Loretto-Eugenia. Interview at Women's Theology Center, Boston, February 8, 1989.

Nesiah, Anita. "Armed Conflict: Peace and Justice by Women?" Lecture presented at Bunting Institute, Cambridge, Mass., March 1, 1988.

Suh Kwang Sun. Lecture at School of Theology, Claremont Graduate School, August 1983.

INDEX